## From Stress to Success DVD from Trivium Test Prep

Dear Customer,

Thank you for purchasing from Trivium Test Prep! Whether you're looking to join the military, get into college, or advance your career, we're honored to be a part of your journey.

To show our appreciation (and to help you relieve a little of that test-prep stress), we're offering a **FREE** *From Stress to Success* **DVD** by Trivium Test Prep. Our DVD includes thirty-five test preparation strategies that will help keep you calm and collected before and during your big exam. All we ask is that you email us your feedback and describe your experience with our product. Amazing, awful, or just so-so: we want to hear what you have to say!

To receive your **FREE** *From Stress to Success* **DVD**, please email us at 5star@triviumtestprep. com. Include "Free 5 Star" in the subject line and the following information in your email:

1. The title of the product you purchased.

2. Your rating from 1 – 5 (with 5 being the best).

3. Your feedback about the product, including how our materials helped you meet your goals and ways in which we can improve our products.

4. Your full name and shipping address so we can send your **FREE** *From Stress to Success* **DVD**.

If you have any questions or concerns please feel free to contact me directly.

Thank you, and good luck with your studies!

**Alyssa Wagoner**
Quality Control
alyssa.wagoner@triviumtestprep.com

# ACCUPLACER Study Guide

## Accuplacer Math and Reading Comprehension Exam Prep with Practice Test Questions

# TABLE OF CONTENTS

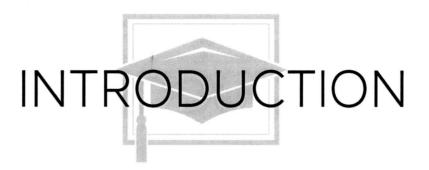

# INTRODUCTION

Congratulations on choosing to take the ACCUPLACER! By purchasing this book, you've taken the first step toward preparing for your college and career goals.

This guide will provide you with a detailed overview of the ACCUPLACER so you know exactly what to expect on test day. We'll take you through all the concepts covered on the test and give you the opportunity to test your knowledge with practice questions. Even if it's been a while since you last took a major test, don't worry; we'll make sure you're more than ready!

## WHAT IS THE ACCUPLACER?

The ACCUPLACER assesses students' abilities in reading, writing and mathematics, helping them prepare for college-level courses. These tests will help you and your academic advisors choose which classes are right for you as you get ready for academic work at the university level.

## WHAT'S ON THE ACCUPLACER?

The ACCUPLACER assesses basic reading comprehension, writing, and arithmetic skills. Depending on a students' abilities on these questions, it will present more difficult questions: college-level mathematics including algebra, coordinate geometry, and trigonometry, and ESL-level comprehension and language skills questions. A student may take any or all of the tests outlined below:

ACCUPLACER outline

| SECTION | CONCEPTS | NUMBER OF QUESTIONS |
|---|---|---|
| Arithmetic | Operations with whole numbers, fractions, decimals, percentages, and applications. | 17 questions |
| College-level math | Algebraic operations and applications; word problems; equations and inequalities; coordinate geometry; trigonometry and functions | 20 questions |
| Elementary algebra | Operations with integers, rational numbers, algebraic expressions; solving equations, inequalities, and word problems | 12 questions |
| Reading comprehension | Main ideas, supporting ideas, drawing inferences, identifying details | 20 questions |

| Sentence skills | Sentence structure and clarity | 20 questions |
| --- | --- | --- |
| WritePlacer (essay) | Effective, organized writing with supported and well-developed ideas, strong sentence structure, and few mechanical errors | 1 essay (300 – 600 words) |
| ESL—language use | Grammar and usage | 20 questions |
| ESL—listening | Comprehension of spoken English | 20 questions |
| ESL—reading skills | Comprehension of English-language reading (short and mid-length passages) | 20 questions |
| ESL—science meaning | Comprehension of English-language sentences | 20 questions |

## HOW IS THE ACCUPLACER SCORED?

The ACCUPLACER is a diagnostic test; as such, it is not scored and there is no way to pass or fail it. This computer-based test adapts to the student's skill level: a student's response to a question determines the difficulty level of the next one.

## HOW IS THE ACCUPLACER ADMINISTERED?

The ACCUPLACER is a multiple-choice test administered by computer. The ESL – Listening section may be administered as a conversation. The exam is not timed. Students must directly contact their college counseling office in order to arrange to take the ACCUPLACER. Your institution's test center will provide information about accommodation for disabilities, required identification or materials, and any options for taking the test remotely.

## HOW DOES THIS BOOK WORK?

The subsequent chapters in this book are divided into those subjects covered on the ACCUPLACER exam. This book is not intended to teach brand-new concepts—there is no way to cram all of that material into one book! Instead, we will help you recall all the information that you've already learned. Even more importantly, we'll show you how to apply that knowledge on the test. Each chapter includes an extensive review, with plenty of examples to make sure you understand the concepts. Finally, you'll have a full practice test at the end so you know for sure you're ready.

Now that you have a firm understanding of the exam and what is included our book, don't forget that learning how to study, as well as how to successfully pass an exam, is just as important as the content. Trivium Test Prep would like to remind you as you begin your studies that we are offering a **FREE** *From Stress to Success* **DVD**. Our DVD includes thirty-five test preparation strategies that will help keep you calm and collected before and during your big exam. All we ask is that you email us your feedback and describe your experience with our product. Amazing, awful, or just so-so: we want to hear what you have to say!

To receive your **FREE** *From Stress to Success* **DVD**, please email us at 5star@triviumtestprep. com. Include

"Free 5 Star" in the subject line and the following information in your email:

1. The title of the product you purchased.
2. Your rating from 1 – 5 (with 5 being the best).
3. Your feedback about the product, including how our materials helped you meet your goals and ways in which we can improve our products.
4. Your full name and shipping address so we can send your **FREE** *From Stress to Success* **DVD**.

We hope you find the rest of this study guide helpful.

# PART I: MATHEMATICS

The ACCUPLACER Mathematics section covers high-school level topics including basic operations, algebra, geometry, statistics, and probability. Most questions will cover algebraic topics, including setting up and solving a variety of equations and inequalities; you'll likely see only a few questions on statistics and probability. The section includes forty multiple-choice questions and twelve gridded-response questions.

## STRATEGIES FOR THE MATHEMATICS SECTION

### Go Back to the Basics

First and foremost, practice your basic skills: sign changes, order of operations, simplifying fractions, and equation manipulation. These are the skills used most on the ACCUPLACER, though they are applied in different contexts. Remember that when it comes down to it, all math problems rely on the four basic skills of addition, subtraction, multiplication, and division. All you need to figure out is the order in which they're used to solve a problem.

### Don't Rely on Mental Math

Using mental math is great for eliminating answer choices, but ALWAYS WRITE DOWN YOUR WORK! This cannot be stressed enough. Use whatever paper is provided; by writing and/or drawing out the problem, you are more likely to catch any mistakes. The act of writing things down also forces you to organize your calculations, leading to an improvement in your ACCUPLACER score.

### The Three-Times Rule

You should read each question at least three times to ensure you're using the correct information and answering the right question:

> Step One: Read the question and write out the given information.

> Step Two: Read the question, set up your equation(s), and solve.

> Step Three: Read the question and check that your answer makes sense (is the amount too large or small; is the answer in the correct unit of measurement, etc.).

### Make an Educated Guess

Eliminate those answer choices which you are relatively sure are incorrect, and then guess from the remaining choices. Educated guessing is critical to increasing your score.

# NUMBERS AND OPERATIONS

The ACCUPLACER will test your abilities to solve problems and perform operations that require basic arithmetic concepts. These include operations with whole numbers and fractions, including estimating and recognizing mixed numbers and equivalent fractions; operations with decimals and percentages, including fraction and percent equivalencies, word problems and estimating; and problem solving through word problems and simple geometry. A review of the basics follows.

## TYPES OF NUMBERS

INTEGERS are whole numbers, including the counting numbers, the negative counting numbers and zero. 3, 2, 1, 0, −1, −2, −3 are examples of integers. RATIONAL NUMBERS are made by dividing one integer by another integer. They can be expressed as fractions or as decimals. 3 divided by 4 makes the rational number $\frac{3}{4}$ or 0.75. IRRATIONAL NUMBERS are numbers that cannot be written as fractions; they are decimals that go on forever without repeating. The number π (3.14159…) is an example of an irrational number.

IMAGINARY NUMBERS are numbers that, when squared, give a negative result. Imaginary numbers use the symbol i to represent $\sqrt{(-1)}$, so $3i = 3\sqrt{(-1)}$ and $(3i)^2 = -9$. COMPLEX NUMBERS are combinations of real and imaginary numbers, written in the form $a + bi$, where $a$ is the real number and $b$ is the imaginary number. An example of a complex number is $4 + 2i$. When adding complex numbers, add the real and imaginary numbers separately: $(4 + 2i) + (3 + i) = 7 + 3i$.

**Examples**

Is $\sqrt{5}$ a rational or irrational number?

> $\sqrt{5}$ is an **irrational number** because it cannot be written as a fraction of two integers. It is a decimal that goes on forever without repeating.

What kind of number is $-\sqrt{64}$?

> $-\sqrt{64}$ can be rewritten as the negative whole number $-8$, so it is an **integer**.

Solve $(3 + 5i) - (1 - 2i)$

> Subtract the real and imaginary numbers separately.
> $3 - 1 = 2$
> $5i - (-2i) = 5i + 2i = 7i$
> So $(3 + 5i) - (1 - 2i) = $ **$2 + 7i$**

# WORKING WITH POSITIVE AND NEGATIVE NUMBERS

Adding, multiplying, and dividing numbers can yield positive or negative values depending on the signs of the original numbers. Knowing these rules can help determine if your answer is correct.

> $(+) + (-) = $ the sign of the larger number
>
> $(-) + (-) = $ negative number
>
> $(-) \times (-) = $ positive number
>
> $(-) \times (+) = $ negative number
>
> $(-) \div (-) = $ positive number
>
> $(-) \div (+) = $ negative number

**Examples**

Find the product of $-10$ and $47$.

> $(-) \times (+) = (-)$
> $-10 \times 47 = $ **$-470$**

What is the sum of $-65$ and $-32$?

> $(-) + (-) = (-)$
> $-65 + -32 = $ **$-97$**

Is the product of $-7$ and $4$ less than $-7$, between $-7$ and $4$, or greater than $4$?

> $(-) \times (+) = (-)$
> $-7 \times 4 = -28$, which is **less than $-7$**

What is the value of −16 divided by 2.5?

$(-) \div (+) = (-)$

$-16 \div 2.5 = \mathbf{-6.4}$

## ORDER OF OPERATIONS

Operations in a mathematical expression are always performed in a specific order, which is described by the acronym PEMDAS:

1. Parentheses
2. Exponents
3. Multiplication
4. Division
5. Addition
6. Subtraction

Perform the operations within parentheses first, and then address any exponents. After those steps, perform all multiplication and division. These are carried out from left to right as they appear in the problem. Finally, do all required addition and subtraction, also from left to right as each operation appears in the problem.

### Examples

Solve: $[-(2)^2 - (4 + 7)]$

First, complete operations within parentheses:

$-(2)^2 - (11)$

Second, calculate the value of exponential numbers:

$-(4) - (11)$

Finally, do addition and subtraction:

$-4 - 11 = \mathbf{-15}$

Solve: $(5)^2 \div 5 + 4 \times 2$

First, calculate the value of exponential numbers:

$(25) \div 5 + 4 \times 2$

Second, calculate division and multiplication from left to right:

$5 + 8$

Finally, do addition and subtraction:

$5 + 8 = \mathbf{13}$

Solve the expression: $15 \times (4 + 8) - 3^3$

First, complete operations within parentheses:

$15 \times (12) - 3^3$

Second, calculate the value of exponential numbers:

$15 \times (12) - 27$

Third, calculate division and multiplication from left to right:

$180 - 27$

Finally, do addition and subtraction from left to right:

$180 - 27 = \mathbf{153}$

Solve the expression: $\left(\frac{5}{2} \times 4\right) + 23 - 4^2$

First, complete operations within parentheses:

$(10) + 23 - 4^2$

Second, calculate the value of exponential numbers:

$(10) + 23 - 16$

Finally, do addition and subtraction from left to right:

$(10) + 23 - 16$

$33 - 16 = \mathbf{17}$

## UNITS OF MEASUREMENT

You are expected to memorize some units of measurement. These are given below. When doing unit conversion problems (i.e., when converting one unit to another), find the conversion factor, then apply that factor to the given measurement to find the new units.

Table 1.1. Unit Prefixes

| PREFIX | SYMBOL | MULTIPLICATION FACTOR |
|---|---|---|
| tera | T | 1,000,000,000,000 |
| giga | G | 1,000,000,000 |
| mega | M | 1,000,000 |
| kilo | k | 1,000 |
| hecto | h | 100 |
| deca | da | 10 |
| base unit | -- | -- |
| deci | d | 0.1 |
| centi | c | 0.01 |
| milli | m | 0.001 |
| micro | μ | 0.0000001 |
| nano | n | 0.0000000001 |
| pico | p | 0.0000000000001 |

Table 1.2. Units and Conversion Factors

| DIMENSION | AMERICAN | SI |
|---|---|---|
| length | inch/foot/yard/mile | meter |
| mass | ounce/pound/ton | gram |
| volume | cup/pint/quart/gallon | liter |
| force | pound-force | newton |
| pressure | pound-force per square inch | pascal |
| work and energy | cal/British thermal unit | joule |

| temperature | Fahrenheit | kelvin |
|---|---|---|
| charge | faraday | coulomb |

## CONVERSION FACTORS

| | |
|---|---|
| 1 in = 2.54 cm | 1 lb = 0.454 kg |
| 1 yd = 0.914 m | 1 cal = 4.19 J |
| 1 mi = 1.61 km | 1 °F = 5/9 (°F − 32) |
| 1 gal = 3.785 L | 1 cm³ = 1 mL |
| 1 oz = 28.35 g | 1 hr = 3600 s |

## Examples

A fence measures 15 ft. long. How many yards long is the fence?

1 yd. = 3 ft.

$\frac{15}{3}$ = **5 yd.**

A pitcher can hold 24 cups. How many gallons can it hold?

1 gal. = 16 cups

$\frac{24}{16}$ = **1.5 gallons**

A spool of wire holds 144 in. of wire. If Mario has 3 spools, how many feet of wire does he have?

12 in. = 1 ft.

$\frac{144}{12}$ = 12 ft.

12 ft. × 3 spools = **36 ft. of wire**

A ball rolling across a table travels 6 inches per second. How many feet will it travel in 1 minute?

This problem can be worked in two steps: finding how many inches are covered in 1 minute, and then converting that value to feet. It can also be worked the opposite way, by finding how many feet it travels in 1 second and then converting that to feet traveled per minute. The first method is shown below.

1 min. = 60 sec.

(6 in.)/(sec.) × 60 s = 360 in.

1 ft. = 12 in.

(360 in.)/(12 in.) = **30 ft.**

How many millimeters are in 0.5 m?

1 meter = 1000 mm

0.5 meters = **500 mm**

A lead ball weighs 38 g. How many kilograms does it weigh?

1 kg = 1000 g

$\frac{38}{1000}$ g = **0.038 kg**

How many cubic centimeters are in 10 L?

    1 L = 1000
    10 L = 1000 × 10
    10 L = **10,000**


Jennifer's pencil was initially 10 centimeters long. After she sharpened it, it was 9.6 centimeters long. How many millimeters did she lose from her pencil by sharpening it?

    1 cm = 10 mm
    10 cm − 9.6 cm = 0.4 cm lost
    0.4 cm = 10 × .4 mm = **4 mm were lost**

## DECIMALS AND FRACTIONS

### Adding and Subtracting Decimals

When adding and subtracting decimals, line up the numbers so that the decimals are aligned. You want to subtract the ones place from the ones place, the tenths place from the tenths place, etc.

**Examples**

Find the sum of 17.07 and 2.52.

    17.07
    +  2.52
    = **19.59**


Jeannette has 7.4 gallons of gas in her tank. After driving, she has 6.8 gallons. How many gallons of gas did she use?

    7.4
    − 6.8
    = **0.6 gal.**

### Multiplying and Dividing Decimals

When multiplying decimals, start by multiplying the numbers normally. You can then determine the placement of the decimal point in the result by adding the number of digits after the decimal in each of the numbers you multiplied together.

When dividing decimals, you should move the decimal point in the divisor (the number you're dividing by) until it is a whole. You can then move the decimal in the dividend (the number you're dividing into) the same number of places in the same direction. Finally, divide the new numbers normally to get the correct answer.

## Examples

What is the product of 0.25 and 1.4?

$25 \times 14 = 350$

There are 2 digits after the decimal in 0.25 and one digit after the decimal in 1.4. Therefore the product should have 3 digits after the decimal: **0.350** is the correct answer.

Find $0.8 \div 0.2$.

Change 0.2 to 2 by moving the decimal one space to the right.

Next, move the decimal one space to the right on the dividend. 0.8 becomes 8.

Now, divide 8 by 2. $8 \div 2 = $ **4**

Find the quotient when 40 is divided by 0.25.

First, change the divisor to a whole number: 0.25 becomes 25.

Next, change the dividend to match the divisor by moving the decimal two spaces to the right, so 40 becomes 4000.

Now divide: $4000 \div 25 = $ **160**

## Working with Fractions

FRACTIONS are made up of two parts: the NUMERATOR, which appears above the bar, and the DENOMINATOR, which is below it. If a fraction is in its SIMPLEST FORM, the numerator and the denominator share no common factors. A fraction with a numerator larger than its denominator is an IMPROPER FRACTION; when the denominator is larger, it's a PROPER FRACTION.

Improper fractions can be converted into proper fractions by dividing the numerator by the denominator. The resulting whole number is placed to the left of the fraction, and the remainder becomes the new numerator; the denominator does not change. The new number is called a MIXED NUMBER because it contains a whole number and a fraction. Mixed numbers can be turned into improper fractions through the reverse process: multiply the whole number by the denominator and add the numerator to get the new numerator.

## Examples

Simplify the fraction $\frac{121}{77}$.

121 and 77 share a common factor of 11. So, if we divide each by 11 we can simplify the fraction:

$$\frac{121}{77} = \frac{11}{11} \times \frac{11}{7} = \frac{11}{7}$$

Convert $\frac{37}{5}$ into a proper fraction.

Start by dividing the numerator by the denominator:

$37 \div 5 = 7$ with a remainder of 2

Now build a mixed number with the whole number and the new numerator:

$$\frac{37}{5} = 7\frac{2}{5}$$

## Multiplying and Dividing Fractions

To multiply fractions, convert any mixed numbers into improper fractions and multiply the numerators together and the denominators together. Reduce to lowest terms if needed.

To divide fractions, first convert any mixed fractions into single fractions. Then, invert the second fraction so that the denominator and numerator are switched. Finally, multiply the numerators together and the denominators together.

Inverting a fraction changes multiplication to division:
$\frac{a}{b} \div \frac{c}{d} = \frac{a}{b} \times \frac{d}{c} = \frac{ad}{bc}$

### Examples

What is the product of $\frac{1}{12}$ and $\frac{6}{8}$?

Simply multiply the numerators together and the denominators together, then reduce:

$$\frac{1}{12} \times \frac{6}{8} = \frac{6}{96} = \frac{1}{16}$$

Sometimes it's easier to reduce fractions before multiplying if you can:

$$\frac{1}{12} \times \frac{6}{8} = \frac{1}{12} \times \frac{3}{4} = \frac{3}{48} = \frac{1}{16}$$

Find $\frac{7}{8} \div \frac{1}{4}$.

For a fraction division problem, invert the second fraction and then multiply and reduce:

$$\frac{7}{8} \div \frac{1}{4} = \frac{7}{8} \times \frac{4}{1} = \frac{28}{8} = \frac{7}{2}$$

The quotient is the result you get when you divide two numbers.

What is the quotient of $\frac{2}{5} \div 1\frac{1}{5}$?

This is a fraction division problem, so the first step is to convert the mixed number to an improper fraction:

$$1\frac{1}{5} = \frac{5 \times 1}{5} + \frac{1}{5} = \frac{6}{5}$$

Now, divide the fractions. Remember to invert the second fraction, and then multiply normally:

$$\frac{2}{5} \div \frac{6}{5} = \frac{2}{5} \times \frac{5}{6} = \frac{10}{30} = \frac{1}{3}$$

A recipe calls for $\frac{1}{4}$ cup of sugar. If 8.5 batches of the recipe are needed, how many cups of sugar will be used?

This is a fraction multiplication problem: $\frac{1}{4} \times 8\frac{1}{2}$.

First, we need to convert the mixed number into a proper fraction:

$$8\frac{1}{2} = \frac{8 \times 2}{2} + \frac{1}{2} = \frac{17}{2}$$

Now, multiply the fractions across the numerators and denominators, and then reduce:

$$\frac{1}{4} \times 8\frac{1}{2} = \frac{1}{4} \times \frac{17}{2} = \mathbf{\frac{17}{8}} \textbf{ cups of sugar}$$

## Adding and Subtracting Fractions

Adding and subtracting fractions requires a COMMON DENOMINATOR. To find the common denominator, you can multiply each fraction by the number 1. With fractions, any number over itself (e.g., $\frac{5}{5}, \frac{12}{12}$, etc.) is equivalent to 1, so multiplying by such a fraction can change the denominator without changing the value of the fraction. Once the denominators are the same, the numerators can be added or subtracted.

To add mixed numbers, you can first add the whole numbers and then the fractions. To subtract mixed numbers, convert each number to an improper fraction, then subtract the numerators.

### Examples

Simplify the expression $\frac{2}{3} - \frac{1}{5}$.

First, multiply each fraction by a factor of 1 to get a common denominator. How do you know which factor of 1 to use? Look at the other fraction and use the number found in that denominator:

$$\frac{2}{3} - \frac{1}{5} = \frac{2}{3}\left(\frac{5}{5}\right) - \frac{1}{5}\left(\frac{3}{3}\right) = \frac{10}{15} - \frac{3}{15}$$

Once the fractions have a common denominator, simply subtract the numerators:

$$\frac{10}{15} - \frac{3}{15} = \mathbf{\frac{7}{15}}$$

Find $2\frac{1}{3} - \frac{3}{2}$.

This is a problem with a mixed number, so the first step is to convert the mixed number to an improper fraction:

$$2\frac{1}{3} = \frac{2 \times 3}{3} + \frac{1}{3} = \frac{7}{3}$$

Next, convert each fraction so they share a common denominator:

$$\frac{7}{3} \times \frac{2}{2} = \frac{14}{6}$$

$$\frac{3}{2} \times \frac{3}{3} = \frac{9}{6}$$

Now, subtract the fractions by subtracting the numerators:

$$\frac{14}{6} - \frac{9}{6} = \mathbf{\frac{5}{6}}$$

The phrase *simplify the expression* just means you need to perform all the operations in the expression.

CONTINUE

Find the sum of $\frac{9}{16}$, $\frac{1}{2}$, and $\frac{7}{4}$.

For this fraction addition problem, we need to find a common denominator. Notice that 2 and 4 are both factors of 16, so 16 can be the common denominator:

$$\frac{1}{2} \times \frac{8}{8} = \frac{8}{16}$$

$$\frac{7}{4} \times \frac{4}{4} = \frac{28}{16}$$

$$\frac{9}{16} + \frac{8}{16} + \frac{28}{16} = \mathbf{\frac{45}{16}}$$

Sabrina has $\frac{2}{3}$ of a can of red paint. Her friend Amos has $\frac{1}{6}$ of a can. How much red paint do they have combined?

To add fractions, make sure that they have a common denominator. Since 3 is a factor of 6, 6 can be the common denominator:

$$\frac{2}{3} \times \frac{2}{2} = \frac{4}{6}$$

Now, add the numerators:

$$\frac{4}{6} + \frac{1}{6} = \mathbf{\frac{5}{6}} \textbf{ of a can}$$

## Converting Fractions to Decimals

Calculators are not allowed on the Accuplacer, which can make handling fractions and decimals intimidating for many test-takers. However, there are several techniques you can use to help you convert between the two forms.

The first thing to do is simply memorize common decimals and their fractional equivalents; a list of these is given below. With these values, it's possible to convert more complicated fractions as well. For example, $\frac{2}{5}$ is just $\frac{1}{5}$ multiplied by 2, so $\frac{2}{5} = 0.2 \times 2 = 0.4$.

Table 1.3. Common Decimals and Fractions

| FRACTION | DECIMAL |
|----------|---------|
| $\frac{1}{2}$ | 0.5 |
| $\frac{1}{3}$ | $0.\overline{33}$ |
| $\frac{1}{4}$ | 0.25 |
| $\frac{1}{5}$ | 0.2 |
| $\frac{1}{6}$ | $0.1\overline{66}$ |
| $\frac{1}{7}$ | $0.\overline{142857}$ |
| $\frac{1}{8}$ | 0.125 |
| $\frac{1}{9}$ | $0.\overline{11}$ |
| $\frac{1}{10}$ | 0.1 |

Knowledge of common decimal equivalents to fractions can also help you estimate. This skill can be particularly helpful on multiple-choice tests like the Accuplacer, where excluding incorrect answers can be just as helpful as knowing how to find the right one. For example, to find in decimal form for an answer, you can eliminate any answers less than 0.5 because $\frac{4}{8}$ = 0.5. You may also know that $\frac{6}{8}$ is the same as $\frac{3}{4}$ or 0.75, so anything above 0.75 can be eliminated as well.

Another helpful trick can be used if the denominator is easily divisible by 100: in the fraction $\frac{9}{20}$, you know 20 goes into 100 five times, so you can multiply the top and bottom by 5 to get $\frac{45}{100}$ or 0.45.

If none of these techniques work, you'll need to find the decimal by dividing the denominator by the numerator using long division.

### Examples

Write $\frac{8}{18}$ as a decimal.

The first step here is to simplify the fraction:

$$\frac{8}{18} = \frac{4}{9}$$

Now it's clear that the fraction is a multiple of $\frac{1}{9}$, so you can easily find the decimal using a value you already know:

$$\frac{4}{9} = \frac{1}{9} \times 4 = 0.\overline{11} \times 4 = \mathbf{0.\overline{44}}$$

Write the fraction $\frac{3}{16}$ as a decimal.

None of the tricks above will work for this fraction, so you need to do long division:

```
        0.1875
  16 ) 3.0000
      - 1 6
        1 40
      - 1 28
          120
       -  112
            80
         -  80
             0
```

$$\frac{3}{16} = \mathbf{0.1875}$$

### Converting Decimals to Fractions

Converting a decimal into a fraction is more straightforward than the reverse process. To convert a decimal, simply use the numbers that come after the decimal as the numerator in the fraction. The denominator will be a power of 10 that matches the place value for the original decimal. For example, the numerator for 0.46 would be 100 because the last number is in the tenths place; likewise, the denominator for 0.657 would be 1000 because the last number is in the thousandths place. Once this fraction has been set up, all that's left is to simplify it.

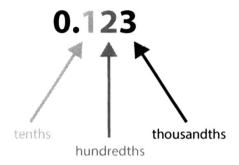

*Figure 1.1. Decimal Places*

**Example**

Convert 0.45 into a fraction.

The last number in the decimal is in the hundredths place, so we can easily set up a fraction:

$0.45 = \frac{45}{100}$

The next step is to simply reduce the fraction down to the lowest common denominator. Here, both 45 and 100 are divisible by 5: 45 divided by 5 is 9, and 100 divided by 5 is 20. Therefore, you're left with:

$\frac{45}{100} = \mathbf{\frac{9}{20}}$

# RATIOS

A **RATIO** tells you how many of one thing exists in relation to the number of another thing. Unlike fractions, ratios do not give a part relative to a whole; instead, they compare two values. For example, if you have 3 apples and 4 oranges, the ratio of apples to oranges is 3 to 4. Ratios can be written using words (3 to 4), fractions ($\frac{3}{4}$), or colons (3:4).

In order to work with ratios, it's helpful to rewrite them as a fraction expressing a part to a whole. For example, in the example above you have 7 total pieces of fruit, so the fraction of your fruit that are apples is $\frac{3}{7}$, and oranges make up $\frac{4}{7}$ of your fruit collection.

One last important thing to consider when working with ratios is the units of the values being compared. On the Accuplacer, you may be asked to rewrite a ratio using the same units on both sides. For example, you might have to rewrite the ratio 3 minutes to 7 seconds as 180 seconds to 7 seconds.

**Examples**

There are 90 voters in a room, and each is either a Democrat or a Republican. The ratio of Democrats to Republicans is 5:4.

How many Republicans are there?

We know that there are 5 Democrats for every 4 Republicans in the room, which means for every 9 people, 4 are Republicans.

$5 + 4 = 9$

Fraction of Democrats: $\frac{5}{9}$

Fraction of Republicans: $\frac{4}{9}$

If $\frac{4}{9}$ of the 90 voters are Republicans, then:

$\frac{4}{9} \times 90 =$ **40 voters are Republicans**

The ratio of students to teachers in a school is 15:1. If there are 38 teachers, how many students attend the school?

To solve this ratio problem, we can simply multiply both sides of the ratio by the desired value to find the number of students that correspond to having 38 teachers:

$\frac{15 \text{ students}}{1 \text{ teacher}} \times 38 = \frac{570 \text{ students}}{38 \text{ teachers}}$

The school has **570 students**.

## PROPORTIONS

A **PROPORTION** is an equation which states that 2 ratios are equal. Proportions are usually written as 2 fractions joined by an equal sign $\left(\frac{a}{b} = \frac{c}{d}\right)$, but they can also be written using colons (a : b :: c : d). Note that in a proportion, the units must be the same in both numerators and in both denominators.

Often you will be given 3 of the values in a proportion and asked to find the 4th. In these types of problems, you can solve for the missing variable by cross-multiplying—multiply the numerator of each fraction by the denominator of the other to get an equation with no fractions as shown below. You can then solve the equation using basic algebra. (For more on solving basic equations, see *Algebraic Expressions and Equations*.)

$$\frac{a}{b} = \frac{c}{d} \rightarrow ad = bc$$

### Examples

A train traveling 120 miles takes 3 hours to get to its destination. How long will it take for the train to travel 180 miles?

Start by setting up the proportion:

$\frac{120 \text{ mi.}}{3 \text{ hr.}} = \frac{180 \text{ mi.}}{x \text{ hr.}}$

Note that it doesn't matter which value is placed in the numerator or denominator, as long as it is the same on both sides. Now, solve for the missing quantity through cross–multiplication:

Ratio and proportion problems are among the most common on the Accuplacer.

$120 \text{ mi.} \times x \text{ hr.} = 3 \text{ hr.} \times 180 \text{ mi.}$

Now solve the equation:

$$x \text{ hr.} = \frac{(3 \text{ hr.}) \times (180 \text{ mi.})}{120 \text{ mi.}} = \mathbf{4.5 \text{ hr.}}$$

One acre of wheat requires 500 gallons of water. How many acres can be watered with 2600 gallons?

Set up the equation:

$$\frac{1 \text{ acre}}{500 \text{ gal.}} = \frac{x \text{ acres}}{2600 \text{ gal.}}$$

Then solve for $x$:

$$x \text{ acres} = \frac{1 \text{ acre} \times 2600 \text{ gal.}}{500 \text{ gal.}}$$

$$x = \frac{26}{5} \text{ or } \mathbf{5.2 \text{ acres}}$$

If $35 : 5 :: 49 : x$, find $x$.

This problem presents two equivalent ratios that can be set up in a fraction equation:

$$\frac{35}{5} = \frac{49}{x}$$

You can then cross-multiply to solve for $x$:

$$35x = 49 \times 5$$

$$x = \mathbf{7}$$

## PERCENTAGES

A **PERCENT** is the ratio of a part to the whole. Questions may give the part and the whole and ask for the percent, or give the percent and the whole and ask for the part, or give the part and the percent and ask for the value of the whole. The equation for percentages can be rearranged to solve for any of these:

$$percent = \frac{part}{whole}$$

$$part = whole \times percent$$

$$whole = \frac{part}{percent}$$

In the equations above, the percent should always be expressed as a decimal. In order to convert a decimal into a percentage value, simply multiply it by 100. So, If you've read 5 pages (the part) of a 10 page article (the whole), you've read $\frac{5}{10} = 0.5$ or 50%. (The percent sign (%) is used once the decimal has been multiplied by 100.)

Note that when solving these problems, the units for the part and the whole should be the same. If you're reading a book, saying you've read 5 pages out of 15 chapters doesn't make any sense.

The word *of* usually indicates what the whole is in a problem. For example, the problem might say *Ella ate 2 slices of the pizza*, which means the pizza is the whole.

## Examples

45 is 15% of what number?

> Set up the appropriate equation and solve. Don't forget to change 15% to a decimal value:
>
> $$whole = \frac{part}{percent} = \frac{45}{0.15} = \textbf{300}$$

Jim spent 30% of his paycheck at the fair. He spent $15 for a hat, $30 for a shirt, and $20 playing games. How much was his check? (Round to nearest dollar.)

> Set up the appropriate equation and solve:
>
> $$whole = \frac{part}{percent} = \frac{15 + 30 + 20}{.30} = \textbf{\$217.00}$$

What percent of 65 is 39?

> Set up the equation and solve:
>
> $$percent = \frac{part}{whole} = \frac{39}{65} = \textbf{0.6 or 60\%}$$

Parvarti and Mario sell cable subscriptions. In a given month, Parvarti sells 45 subscriptions and Mario sells 51. If 240 total subscriptions were sold in that month, what percent were not sold by Parvarti or Mario?

> You can use the information in the question to figure out what percentage of subscriptions were sold by Parvarti and Mario:
>
> $$percent = \frac{part}{whole} = \frac{(51 + 45)}{240} = 96/240 = 0.4 \text{ or } 40\%$$
>
> However, the question asks how many subscriptions weren't sold by Mario or Parvarti. If they sold 40%, then the other salespeople sold 100% − 40% = **60%**.

Grant needs to score 75% on an exam. If the exam has 45 questions, at least how many does he need to answer correctly?

> Set up the equation and solve. Remember to convert 75% to a decimal value:
>
> $part = whole \times percent = 45 \times 0.75 = 33.75$, so he needs to answer at least **34 questions correctly**.

## Percent Change

PERCENT CHANGE problems will ask you to calculate how much a given quantity changed. The problems are solved in a similar way as regular percent problems, except that instead of using the *part* you'll use the *amount of change*. Note that the sign of the *amount of change* is important: if the original amount has increased the change will be positive, and if it has decreased the change will be negative. Again, in the equations below the percent is a decimal value; you need to multiply by 100 to get the actual percentage.

$$percent\ change = \frac{amount\ of\ change}{original\ amount}$$

$$amount\ of\ change = original\ amount \times percent\ change$$

$$original\ amount = \frac{amount\ of\ change}{percent\ change}$$

## Examples

A computer software retailer marks up its games by 40% above the wholesale price when it sells them to customers. Find the price of a game for a customer if the game cost the retailer $25.

Set up the appropriate equation and solve:

*amount of change = original amount × percent change*

$25 \times 0.4 = 10$

If the amount of change is 10, that means the store adds a markup of $10, so the game costs:

$25 + $10 = **$35**

A golf shop pays its wholesaler $40 for a certain club, and then sells it to a golfer for $75. What is the markup rate?

First, calculate the amount of change:

$75 - 40 = 35$

Now you can set up the equation and solve. (Note that *markup rate* is another way of saying *percent change*):

$$percent\ change = \frac{amount\ of\ change}{original\ amount} = \frac{35}{40} = 0.875 = \mathbf{87.5\%}$$

A store charges a 40% markup on the shoes it sells. How much did the store pay for a pair of shoes purchased by a customer for $63?

You're solving for the original price, but it's going to be tricky because you don't know the amount of change; you only know the new price. To solve, you need to create an expression for the amount of change:

If *original amount* = $x$

Then *amount of change* = $63 - x$

Now you can plug these values into your equation:

*original amount = amount of change ÷ percent change*

$x = \frac{63 - x}{0.4}$

The last step is to solve for $x$:

$0.4x = 63 - x$

$1.4x = 63$

$x = 45$

The store paid **$45** for the shoes.

An item originally priced at $55 is marked 25% off. What is the sale price?

> You've been asked to find the sale price, which means you need to solve for the amount of change first:
>
> *amount of change = original amount × percent change*
>
> $= 55 \times 0.25 = 13.75$
>
> Using this amount, you can find the new price. Because it's on sale, we know the item will cost less than the original price:
>
> $55 - 13.75 = 41.25$
>
> The sale price is **$41.25**.

James wants to put in an 18 foot by 51 foot garden in his backyard. If he does, it will reduce the size of his yard by 24%. What will be the area of the remaining yard?

> This problem is tricky because you need to figure out what each number in the problem stands for. 24% is obviously the percent change, but what about the measurements in feet? If you multiply these values you get the area of the garden (for more on area see *Area and Perimeter*):
>
> $18 \text{ ft.} \times 51 \text{ ft.} = 918 \text{ ft.}^2$
>
> This 918 ft.² is the amount of change—it's how much smaller the lawn is. Now we can set up an equation:
>
> $original\ amount = \dfrac{amount\ of\ change}{percent\ change} = \dfrac{918}{24} = 3825$
>
> If the original lawn was 3825 ft.² and the garden is 918 ft.², then the remaining area is
>
> $3825 - 918 = 2907$
>
> The remaining lawn covers **2907 ft.²**

## COMPARISON OF RATIONAL NUMBERS

Number comparison problems present numbers in different formats and ask which is larger or smaller, or whether the numbers are equivalent. The important step in solving these problems is to convert the numbers to the same format so that it is easier to compare them. If numbers are given in the same format, or after converting them, determine which number is smaller or if the numbers are equal. Remember that for negative numbers, higher numbers are actually smaller.

### Examples

Is $4\frac{3}{4}$ greater than, equal to, or less than $\frac{18}{4}$?

> These numbers are in different formats—one is a mixed fraction and the other is just a fraction. So, the first step is to convert the mixed fraction to a fraction:
>
> $4\frac{3}{4} = 4 \times \frac{4}{4} + \frac{3}{4} = \frac{19}{4}$

Once the mixed number is converted, it is easier to see that $\frac{19}{4}$ **is greater than** $\frac{18}{4}$.

Which of the following numbers has the greatest value: 104.56, 104.5, or 104.6?

These numbers are already in the same format, so the decimal values just need to be compared. Remember that zeros can be added after the decimal without changing the value, so the three numbers can be rewritten as:

104.56

104.50

104.60

From this list, it is clearer to see that 104.60 is the greatest because 0.60 is larger than 0.50 and 0.56.

Is 65% greater than, less than, or equal to $\frac{13}{20}$?

The first step is to convert the numbers into the same format. 65% is the same as $\frac{65}{100}$. Next, the fractions need to be converted to have the same denominator. It is difficult to compare fractions with different denominators. Using a factor of $\frac{5}{5}$ on the second fraction will give common denominators:

$\frac{13}{20} \times \frac{5}{5} = \frac{65}{100}$.

Now, it is easy to see that **the numbers are equivalent**.

## EXPONENTS AND RADICALS

Exponents tell us how many times to multiply a base number by itself. In the example $2^4$, 2 is the base number and 4 is the exponent. $2^4 = 2 \times 2 \times 2 \times 2 = 16$. Exponents are also called powers: 5 to the third power = $5^3 = 5 \times 5 \times 5 = 125$. Some exponents have special names: $x$ to the second power is also called "$x$ squared" and $x$ to the third power is also called "$x$ cubed." The number 3 squared = $3^2 = 3 \times 3 = 9$.

Radicals are expressions that use roots. Radicals are written in the form $\sqrt(a \,\&\, x)$, where $a$ = the radical power and $x$ = the radicand. The solution to the radical ⊠8 is the number that, when multiplied by itself 3 times, equals 8. ⊠8 = 2 because $2 \times 2 \times 2 = 8$. When the radical power is not written we assume it is 2, so $\sqrt{9} = 3$ because $3 \times 3 = 9$. Radicals can also be written as exponents, where the power is a fraction. For example, $x^{1/3} = \sqrt[3]{x}$.

Review more of the rules for working with exponents and radicals in the table below.

Table 1.4. Exponents and Radicals Rules

| RULE | EXAMPLE |
|---|---|
| $x^0 = 1$ | $5^0 = 1$ |
| $x^1 = x$ | $5^1 = 5$ |
| $x^a \times x^b = x^{a+b}$ | $5^2 \times 5^3 = 5^5 = 3125$ |
| $(xy)^a = x^a y^a$ | $(5 \times 6)^2 = 5^2 \times 6^2 = 900$ |
| $(x^a)^b = x^{ab}$ | $(5^2)^3 = 5^6 = 15{,}625$ |
| $\left(\dfrac{x}{y}\right)^a = \dfrac{x^a}{y^b}$ | $\left(\dfrac{5}{6}\right)^2 = \dfrac{5^2}{6^2} = \dfrac{25}{36}$ |
| $\dfrac{x^a}{x^b} = x^{a-b} \ (x \neq 0)$ | $\dfrac{5^4}{5^3} = 5^1 = 5$ |
| $x^{-a} = \dfrac{1}{x^a} \ (x \neq 0)$ | $5^{-2} = \dfrac{1}{5^2} = \dfrac{1}{25}$ |
| $x^{\frac{1}{a}} = \sqrt[a]{x}$ | $25^{\frac{1}{2}} = \sqrt[2]{25} = 5$ |
| $\sqrt[a]{x \times y} = \sqrt[a]{x} \times \sqrt[a]{y}$ | $\sqrt[3]{8 \times 27} = \sqrt[3]{8} \times \sqrt[3]{27} = 2 \times 3 = 6$ |
| $\sqrt[a]{\dfrac{x}{y}} = \dfrac{\sqrt[a]{x}}{\sqrt[a]{y}}$ | $\sqrt[3]{\dfrac{27}{8}} = \dfrac{\sqrt[3]{27}}{\sqrt[3]{8}} = \dfrac{3}{2}$ |
| $\sqrt[a]{x^b} = x^{\frac{b}{a}}$ | $\sqrt[2]{5^4} = 5^{\frac{4}{2}} = 5^2 = 25$ |

## Examples

Simplify the expression $2^4 \times 2^2$

> When multiplying exponents in which the base number is the same, simply add the powers:
>
> $2^4 \times 2^2 = 2^{(4+2)} = 2^6$
>
> $2^6 = 2 \times 2 \times 2 \times 2 \times 2 \times 2 = \textbf{64}$

Simplify the expression $(3^4)^{-1}$

> When an exponent is raised to a power, multiply the powers:
>
> $(3^4)^{-1} = 3^{-4}$
>
> When the exponent is a negative number, rewrite as the reciprocal of the positive exponent:
>
> $3^{-4} = \dfrac{1}{3^4}$
>
> $\dfrac{1}{3^4} = \dfrac{1}{3 \times 3 \times 3 \times 3} = \dfrac{\textbf{1}}{\textbf{81}}$

CONTINUE

Simplify the expression $\left(\dfrac{9}{4}\right)^{\frac{1}{2}}$

When the power is a fraction, rewrite as a radical:

$$\left(\frac{9}{4}\right)^{\frac{1}{2}} = \sqrt{\frac{9}{4}}$$

Next, distribute the radical to the numerator and denominator:

$$\sqrt{\frac{9}{4}} = \frac{\sqrt{9}}{\sqrt{4}} = \frac{3}{2}$$

# 2

# ALGEBRA

The ACCUPLACER includes both an Elementary Algebra test and also a College-Level Math test that contains questions on algebraic expressions, equations, inequalities, and functions.

The Elementary Algebra test will cover integers, absolute value, simple expressions, monomials and polynomials, simplifying algebraic fractions, factoring, solving equations and inequalities, and solving word problems. Review linear equations and quadratic equations as well as strategies for word problems.

The algebraic components of the College-Level Math Test include simplifying expressions, factoring, and working with exponents and roots. Prepare to solve systems of equations, linear and quadratic equations and others. Also prepare for complex word problems.

## ALGEBRAIC EXPRESSIONS

Algebraic expressions and equations include **VARIABLES**, or letters standing in for numbers. These expressions and equations are made up of terms, which are groups of numbers and variables (e.g., $2xy$). An **EXPRESSION** is simply a set of terms (e.g., $\frac{2x}{3yz} + 2$). When those terms are joined only by addition or subtraction, the expression is called a **POLYNOMIAL** (e.g., $2x + 3yz$). When working with expressions, you'll need to use many different mathematical properties and operations, including addition/subtraction, multiplication/division, exponents, roots, distribution, and the order of operations.

### Evaluating Algebraic Expressions

To evaluate an algebraic expression, simply plug the given value(s) in for the appropriate variable(s) in the expression.

> **Example**
>
> Evaluate $2x + 6y - 3z$ if $x = 2$, $y = 4$, and $z = -3$.
>
> Plug in each number for the correct variable and simplify:
>
> $2x + 6y - 3z = 2(2) + 6(4) - 3(-3) = 4 + 24 + 9 = \mathbf{37}$

## Adding and Subtracting Expressions

Only LIKE TERMS, which have the exact same variable(s), can be added or subtracted. CONSTANTS are numbers without variables attached, and those can be added and subtracted together as well. When simplifying an expression, like terms should be added or subtracted so that no individual group of variables occurs in more than one term. For example, the expression $5x + 6xy$ is in its simplest form, while $5x + 6xy - 11xy$ is not because the term $xy$ appears more than once.

> **Examples**
>
> Simplify the expression $5xy + 7y + 2yz + 11xy - 5yz$
>
> Start by grouping together like terms:
>
> $(5xy + 11xy) + (2yz - 5yz) + 7y$
>
> Now you can add together each set of like terms:
>
> $\mathbf{16xy + 7y - 3yz}$

## Multiplying and Dividing Expressions

To multiply a single term by another, simply multiply the coefficients and then multiply the variables. Remember that when multiplying variables with exponents, those exponents are added together. For example, $(x^5y)(x^3y^4) = x^8y^5$.

When multiplying a term by a set of terms inside parentheses, you need to DISTRIBUTE to each term inside the parentheses as shown below:

$$a(b+c) = ab + ac$$

*Figure 2.1. Distribution*

When variables occur in both the numerator and denominator of a fraction, they cancel each other out. So, a fraction with variables in its simplest form will not have the same variable on the top and bottom.

> **Examples**
>
> Simplify the expression $(3x^4y^2z)(2y^4z^5)$.
>
> Multiply the coefficients and variables together:
>
> $3 \times 2 = 6$
>
> $y^2 \times y^4 = y^6$

$z \times z^5 = z^6$

Now put all the terms back together:

**$6x^4y^6z^6$**


Simplify the expression: $(2y^2)(y^3 + 2xy^2z + 4z)$

Multiply each term inside the parentheses by the term $2y^2$:

$(2y^2)(y^3 + 2xy^2z + 4z) =$

$(2y^2 \times y^3) + (2y^2 \times 2xy^2z) \times (2y^2 \times 4z) =$

**$2y^5 + 4xy^4z + 8y^2z$**


Simplify the expression: $(5x + 2)(3x + 3)$

Use the acronym FOIL—first, outer, inner, last—to multiply the terms:

first: $5x \times 3x = 15x^2$

outer: $5x \times 3 = 15x$

inner: $2 \times 3x = 6x$

last: $2 \times 3 = 6$

Now combine like terms:

**$15x^2 + 21x + 6$**


Simplify the expression: $\frac{2x^4y^3z}{8x^2z^2}$

Simplify by looking at each variable and checking for those that appear in the numerator and denominator:

$\frac{2}{8} = \frac{1}{4}$

$\frac{x^4}{x^2} = \frac{x^2}{1}$

$\frac{z}{z^2} = \frac{1}{z}$

$\frac{2x^4y^3z}{8x^2z^2} = \frac{x^2y^3}{4z}$

When multiplying terms, add the exponents. When dividing, subtract the exponents.


## Factoring Expressions

FACTORING is splitting one expression into the multiplication of two expressions. It requires finding the HIGHEST COMMON FACTOR and dividing terms by that number. For example, in the expression $15x + 10$, the highest common factor is 5 because both terms are divisible by 5: $\frac{15x}{5} = 3x$ and $\frac{10}{5} = 2$. When you factor the expression you get $5(3x + 2)$.

Sometimes it is difficult to find the highest common factor. In these cases, consider whether the expression fits a polynomial identity. A POLYNOMIAL is an expression with more than one term. If you can recognize the common polynomials listed below, you can easily factor the expression.

$a^2 - b^2 = (a + b)(a - b)$

$a^2 + 2ab + b^2 = (a + b)(a + b) = (a + b)^2$

$a^2 - 2ab + b^2 = (a - b)(a - b) = (a - b)^2$

$$a^3 + b^3 = (a + b)(a^2 - ab - b^2)$$
$$a^3 - b^3 = (a - b)(a^2 + ab + b^2)$$

**Examples**

Factor the expression $27x^2 - 9x$

First, find the highest common factor. Both terms are divisible by 9:

$\frac{27x^2}{9} = 3x^2$ and $\frac{9x}{9} = x$

Now the expression is $9(3x^2 - x)$ – but wait, you're not done! Both terms can be divided by $x$:

$\frac{3x^2}{x} = 3x$ and $\frac{x}{x} = 1$.

The final factored expression is **$9x(3x - 1)$**.

Factor the expression $25x^2 - 16$

Since there is no obvious factor by which you can divide terms, you should consider whether this expression fits one of your polynomial identities.

This expression is a difference of squares $a^2 - b^2$, where $a^2 = 25x^2$ and $b^2 = 16$.

Recall that $a^2 - b^2 = (a + b)(a - b)$. Now solve for $a$ and $b$:

$a = \sqrt{25x^2} = 5x$

$b = \sqrt{16} = 4$

$(a + b)(a - b) = $ **$(5x + 4)(5x - 4)$**

You can check your work by using the FOIL acronym to expand your answer back to the original expression:

first: $5x \times 5x = 25x^2$

outer: $5x \times -4 = -20x$

inner: $4 \times 5x = 20x$

last: $4 \times -4 = -16$

$25x^2 - 20x + 20x - 16 = 25x^2 - 16$

Factor the expression $100x^2 + 60x + 9$

This is another polynomial identity, $a^2 + 2ab + b^2$. (The more you practice these problems, the faster you will recognize polynomial identities.)

$a^2 = 100x^2$, $2ab = 60x$, and $b^2 = 9$

Recall that $a^2 + 2ab + b^2 = (a + b)^2$. Now solve for $a$ and $b$:

$a = \sqrt{100x^2} = 10x$

$b = \sqrt{9} = 3$

(Double check your work by confirming that $2ab = 2 \times 10x \times 3 = 60x$)

$(a + b)^2 = $ **$(10x + 3)^2$**

# LINEAR EQUATIONS

An **EQUATION** is a statement saying that two expressions are equal to each other. They always include an equal sign (e.g., $3x + 2xy = 17$). A **LINEAR EQUATION** has only two variables; on a graph, linear equations form a straight line.

## Solving Linear Equations

To solve an equation, you need to manipulate the terms on each side to isolate the variable, meaning if you want to find $x$, you have to get the $x$ alone on one side of the equal sign. To do this, you'll need to use many of the tools discussed above: you might need to distribute, divide, add or subtract like terms, or find common denominators.

Think of each side of the equation as the two sides of a see-saw. As long as the two people on each end weigh the same amount (no matter what it is) the see-saw will be balanced: if you have a 120 pound person on each end, the see-saw is balanced. Giving each of them a 10 pound rock to hold changes the weight on each end, but the see-saw itself stays balanced. Equations work the same way: you can add, subtract, multiply, or divide whatever you want as long as you do the same thing to both sides.

Most equations you'll see on the Accuplacer can be solved using the same basic steps:

1. distribute to get rid of parentheses
2. use LCD to get rid of fractions
3. add/subtract like terms on either side
4. add/subtract so that constants appear on only one side of the equation
5. multiply/divide to isolate the variable

### Examples

Solve for $x$: $25x + 12 = 62$

> This equation has no parentheses, fractions, or like terms on the same side, so you can start by subtracting 12 from both sides of the equation:
>
> $25x + 12 = 62$
>
> $(25x + 12) - 12 = 62 - 12$
>
> $25x = 50$
>
> Now, divide by 25 to isolate the variable:
>
> $\frac{25x}{25} = \frac{50}{25}$
>
> $x = 2$

Solve the following equation for $x$: $2x - 4(2x + 3) = 24$

> Start by distributing to get rid of the parentheses (don't forget to distribute the negative):
>
> $2x - 4(2x + 3) = 24$

$2x - 8x - 12 = 24$

There are no fractions, so now you can join like terms:

$2x - 8x - 12 = 24$

$-6x - 12 = 24$

Now add 12 to both sides and divide by −6.

$-6x - 12 = 24$

$(-6x - 12) + 12 = 24 + 12$

$-6x = 36$

$\frac{-6x}{-6} = \frac{36}{-6}$

**$x = -6$**

Solve the following equation for $x$: $\frac{x}{3} + \frac{1}{2} = \frac{x}{6} - \frac{5}{12}$

Start by multiplying by the least common denominator to get rid of the fractions:

$\frac{x}{3} + \frac{1}{2} = \frac{x}{6} - \frac{5}{12}$

$\frac{12x}{3} + \frac{1}{2} = \frac{12x}{6} - \frac{5}{12}$

$4x + 6 = 2x - 5$

Now you can isolate the $x$:

$(4x + 6) - 6 = (2x - 5) - 6 \rightarrow$

$4x = 2x - 11 \rightarrow$

$(4x) - 2x = (2x - 11) - 2x \rightarrow$

$2x = -11$

**$x = -11/2$**

Find the value of $x$: $2(x + y) - 7x = 14x + 3$

This equation looks more difficult because it has 2 variables, but you can use the same steps to solve for $x$. First, distribute to get rid of the parentheses and combine like terms:

$2(x + y) - 7x = 14x + 3 \rightarrow$

$2x + 2y - 7x = 14x + 3 \rightarrow$

$-5x + 2y = 14x + 3$

Now you can move the $x$ terms to one side and everything else to the other, and then divide to isolate $x$:

$-5x + 2y = 14x + 3 \rightarrow$

$-19x = -2y + 3 \rightarrow$

**$x = \frac{2y - 3}{19}$**

## Graphing Linear Equations

Linear equations can be plotted as straight lines on a coordinate plane. The X-AXIS is always the horizontal axis and the Y-AXIS is always the vertical axis. The x-axis is positive to the right of the y-axis and negative to the left. The y-axis is positive above the x-axis and negative below. To describe the location of any point on the graph, write the coordinates in the form $(x, y)$. The origin, the point where the $x$- and $y$-axes cross, is $(0, 0)$.

The **Y-INTERCEPT** is the $y$ coordinate where the line crosses the $y$-axis. The slope is a measure of how steep the line is. **SLOPE** is calculated by dividing the change along the $y$-axis by the change along the $x$-axis between any two points on the line.

Linear equations are easiest to graph when they are written in **POINT-SLOPE FORM**: $y = mx + b$. The constant $m$ represents slope and the constant $b$ represents the $y$-intercept. If you know two points along the line $(x_1, y_1)$ and $(x_2, y_2)$, you can calculate slope using the following equation: $m = \frac{y_2 - y_1}{x_2 - x_1}$. If you know the slope and one other point along the line, you can calculate the $y$-intercept by plugging the number 0 in for $x_2$ and solving for $y_2$.

When graphing a linear equation, first plot the $y$-intercept. Next, plug in values for $x$ to solve for $y$ and plot additional points. Connect the points with a straight line.

## Examples

Find the slope of the line: $\frac{3y}{2} + 3 = x$

Slope is easiest to find when the equation is in point-slope form ($y = mx + b$). Rearrange the equation to isolate $y$:

$\frac{3y}{2} + 3 = x$

$3y + 6 = 2x$

$y + 2 = \frac{2x}{3}$

$y = \frac{2x}{3} - 2$

Finally, identify the term $m$ to find the slope of the line:

$m = \frac{2}{3}$

Plot the linear equation $2y - 4x = 6$

First, rearrange the linear equation to point-slope form ($y = mx + b$):

$2y - 4x = 6$

$y = 2x + 3$

Next, identify the $y$-intercept ($b$) and the slope ($m$):

$b = 3, m = 2$

Now, plot the $y$-intercept $(0, b) = (0, 3)$:

Next, plug in values for $x$ and solve for $y$:

$y = 2(1) + 3 = 5 \rightarrow (1,5)$

$y = 2(-1) + 3 = 1 \rightarrow (-1,1)$

Plot these points on the graph, and connect the points with a straight line:

→

CONTINUE

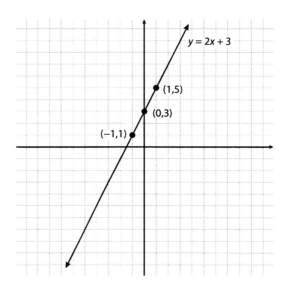

## Systems of Equations

A system of equations is a group of related questions sharing the same variable. The problems you see on the Accuplacer will most likely involve two equations that each have two variables, although you may also solve sets of equations with any number of variables as long as there are a corresponding number of equations (e.g., to solve a system with four variables, you need four equations).

There are two main methods used to solve systems of equations. In SUBSTITUTION, solve one equation for a single variable, then substitute the solution for that variable into the second equation to solve for the other variable. Or, you can use ELIMINATION by adding equations together to cancel variables and solve for one of them.

### Examples

Solve the following system of equations: $3y - 4 + x = 0$ and $5x + 6y = 11$

To solve this system using substitution, first solve one equation for a single variable:

$3y - 4 + x = 0$

$3y + x = 4$

$x = 4 - 3y$

Next, substitute the expression to the right of the equal sign for $x$ in the second equation:

$5x + 6y = 11$

$5(4 - 3y) + 6y = 11$

$20 - 15y + 6y = 11$

$20 - 9y = 11$

$-9y = -9$

$y = 1$

Finally, plug the value for $y$ back into the first equation to find the value of $x$:

$3y - 4 + x = 0$

$3(1) - 4 + x = 0$

$-1 + x = 0$

$x = 1$

The solution is **x = 1** and **y = 1**, or the point **(1, 1)**.

Solve the system $2x + 4y = 8$ and $4x + 2y = 10$

To solve this system using elimination, start by manipulating one equation so that a variable (in this case $x$) will cancel when the equations are added together:

$2x + 4y = 8$

$-2(2x + 4y = 8)$

$-4x - 8y = -16$

Now you can add the two equations together, and the $x$ variable will drop out:

$-4x - 8y = -16$

$\underline{4x + 2y = 10}$

$-6y = -6$

$y = 1$

Lastly, plug the $y$ value into one of the equations to find the value of $x$:

$2x + 4y = 8$

$2x + 4(1) = 8$

$2x + 4 = 8$

$2x = 4$

$x = 2$

The solution is **x = 2** and **y = 1**, or the point **(2, 1)**.

## Building Equations

Word problems describe a situation or a problem without explicitly providing an equation to solve. It is up to you to build an algebraic equation to solve the problem. You must translate the words into mathematical operations. Represent the quantity you do not know with a variable. If there is more than one unknown, you will likely have to write more than one equation, then solve the system of equations by substituting expressions. Make sure you keep your variables straight!

### Examples

David, Jesse and Mark shoveled snow during their snow day and made a total of $100. They agreed to split it based on how much each person worked. David will take $10 more than Jesse, who will take $15 more than Mark. How much money will David get?

Start by building an equation. David's amount will be $d$, Jesse's amount will be $j$, and Mark's amount will be $m$. All three must add up to $100:

$d + j + m = 100$

It may seem like there are three unknowns in this situation, but you can express $j$ and $m$ in terms of $d$:

Jesse gets \$10 less than David, so $j = d - 10$. Mark gets \$15 less than Jesse, so $m = j - 15$.

Substitute the previous expression for $j$ to solve for $m$ in terms of $d$:

$m = (d - 10) - 15 = d - 25$

Now back to our original equation, substituting for $j$ and $m$:

$d + (d - 10) + (d - 25) = 100$

$3d - 35 = 100$

$3d = 135$

$d = 45$

David will get **\$45**.

The sum of three consecutive numbers is 54. What is the middle number?

Start by building an equation. One of the numbers in question will be $x$. The three numbers are consecutive, so if $x$ is the smallest number then the other two numbers must be $(x + 1)$ and $(x - 1)$. You know that the sum of the three numbers is 54:

$x + (x + 1) + (x + 2) = 54$

Now solve for the equation to find $x$:

$3x + 3 = 54$

$3x = 51$

$x = 17$

The question asks about the middle number $(x + 1)$, so the answer is **18**.

Notice that you could have picked any number to be $x$. If you picked the middle number as $x$, your equation would be
$(x - 1) + x + (x + 1) = 54$. Solve for $x$ to get 18.

There are 42 people on the varsity football team. This is 8 more than half the number of people on the swim team. There are 6 fewer boys on the swim team than girls. How many girls are on the swim team?

This word problem might seem complicated at first, but as long as you keep your variables straight and translate the words into mathematical operations you can easily build an equation. The quantity you want to solve is the number of girls on the swim team, so this will be $x$.

The number of boys on the swim team will be $y$. There are 6 fewer boys than girls so $y = x - 6$.

The total number of boys and girls on the swim team is $x + y$.

42 is 8 more than half this number, so $42 = 8 + (x + y) \div 2$

Now substitute for $y$ to solve for $x$:

$42 = 8 + (x + x - 7) \div 2$

$34 = (2x - 6) \div 2$

$68 = 2x - 6$

$74 = 2x$

$x = 37$

There are **37** girls on the swim team.

# LINEAR INEQUALITIES

INEQUALITIES look like equations, except that instead of having an equal sign, they have one of the following symbols:

> greater than: the expression left of the symbol is larger than the expression on the right

< less than: the expression left of the symbol is smaller than the expression on the right

≥ greater than or equal to: the expression left of the symbol is larger than or equal to the expression on the right

≤ less than or equal to: the expression left of the symbol is less than or equal to the expression on the right

## Solving Linear Inequalities

Inequalities are solved like linear and algebraic equations. The only difference is that the symbol must be reversed when both sides of the equation are multiplied by a negative number.

### Examples

Solve for $x$: $-7x + 2 < 6 - 5x$

Collect like terms on each side as you would for a regular equation:

$-7x + 2 < 6 - 5x \rightarrow$

$-2x < 4$

When you divide by a negative number, the direction of the sign switches:

$-2x < 4 \rightarrow$

$x > -2$

See *Solving Linear Equations* for step-by-step instructions on solving basic equations.

## Graphing Linear Inequalities

Graphing a linear inequality is just like graphing a linear equation, except that you shade the area on one side of the line. To graph a linear inequality, first rearrange the inequality expression into $y = mx + b$ form. Then treat the inequality symbol like an equal sign and plot the line. If the inequality symbol is < or >, make a broken line; for ≤ or ≥, make a solid line. Finally, shade the correct side of the graph:

For $y < mx + b$ or $y \leq mx + b$, shade the side below the line.

For $y > mx + b$ or $y \geq mx + b$, shade the side above the line.

### Examples

Plot the inequality $3x \geq 4 - y$

> To rearrange the inequality into $y = mx + b$ form, first subtract 4 from both sides:
>
> $3x - 4 \geq -y$
>
> Next divide both sides by −1 to get positive $y$; remember to switch the direction of the inequality symbol:
>
> $-3x + 4 \leq y$
>
> Now plot the line $y = -3x + 4$, making a solid line:
>
> Finally, shade the side above the line:

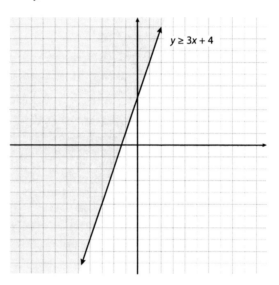

$y \geq 3x + 4$

# QUADRATIC EQUATIONS

A quadratic equation is any equation in the form $ax^2 + bx + c = 0$. In quadratic equations, $x$ is the variable and $a$, $b$, and $c$ are all known numbers. $a$ cannot be 0.

## Solving Quadratic Equations

There is more than one way to solve a quadratic equation. One way is by **FACTORING**. By rearranging the expression $ax^2 + bx + c$ into one factor multiplied by another factor, you can easily solve for the **ROOTS**, the values of $x$ for which the quadratic expression equals 0. Another way to solve a quadratic equation is by using **THE QUADRATIC FORMULA**: $x = \dfrac{-b \pm \sqrt{b^2 - 4ac}}{2a}$. The expression $b^2 - 4ac$ is called the **DISCRIMINANT**; when it is positive you will get two real numbers for $x$, when it is negative you will get one real number and one imaginary number for $x$, and when it is zero you will get one real number for $x$.

### Examples

Factor the quadratic equation $-2x^2 = 14x$ and find the roots.

Not every quadratic equation you see will be presented in the standard form. Rearrange terms to set one side equal to 0:

$2x^2 + 14x = 0$

Note that $a = 2$, $b = 14$, and $c = 0$ because there is no third term.

Now divide the expression on the left by the common factor:

$(2x)(x + 7) = 0$

To find the roots, set each of the factors equal to 0:

$2x = 0 \rightarrow \textbf{\textit{x} = 0}$

$x + 7 = 0 \rightarrow \textbf{\textit{x} = -7}$

Use the quadratic formula to solve for $x$: $3x^2 = 7x - 2$

First rearrange the equation to set one side equal to 0:

$3x^2 - 7x + 2 = 0$

Next identify the terms $a$, $b$, and $c$:

$a = 3, b = -7, c = 2$

Now plug those terms into the quadratic formula:

$x = \dfrac{-b \pm \sqrt{b^2 - 4ac}}{2a}$

$x = \dfrac{7 \pm \sqrt{(-7)^2 - 4(3)(2)}}{2(3)}$

$x = \dfrac{7 \pm \sqrt{25}}{6}$

$x = \dfrac{7 \pm 5}{6}$

Since the determinant is positive, you can expect two real numbers for $x$. Solve for the two possible answers:

$x = \dfrac{7 + 5}{6} \rightarrow \textbf{\textit{x} = 2}$

$x = \dfrac{7 - 5}{6} \rightarrow \textbf{\textit{x} = 1/3}$

## Graphing Quadratic Equations

Graphing a quadratic equation forms a PARABOLA. A parabola is a symmetrical, horseshoe-shaped curve; a vertical axis passes through its vertex. Each term in the equation $ax^2 + bx + c = 0$ affects the shape of the parabola. A bigger value for $a$ makes the curve narrower, while a smaller value makes the curve wider. A negative value for $a$ flips the parabola upside down. The AXIS OF SYMMETRY is the vertical line $x = \frac{-b}{2a}$. To find the $y$-coordinate for the VERTEX, plug this value for $x$ into the expression $ax^2 + bx + c$. The easiest way to graph a quadratic equation is to find the axis of symmetry, solve for the vertex, and then create a table of points by plugging in other numbers for $x$ and solving for $y$. Plot these points and trace the parabola.

## Examples

Graph the equation $x^2 + 4x + 1 = 0$

First, find the axis of symmetry. The equation for the line of symmetry is $x = \frac{-b}{2a}$.

$x = \frac{-4}{2(1)} = -2$

Next, plug in $-2$ for $x$ to find the $y$ coordinate of the vertex:

$y = (-2)^2 + 4(-2) + 1 = -3$

The vertex is $(-2, -3)$

Now, make a table of points on either side of the vertex by plugging in numbers for $x$ and solving for $y$:

| $x$ | $y = x^2 + 4x + 1$ | $(x, y)$ |
|---|---|---|
| −3 | $y = (-3)^2 + 4(-3) + 1 = -2$ | $(-3, -2)$ |
| −1 | $y = (-1)^2 + 4(-1) + 1 = -2$ | $(-1, -2)$ |
| −4 | $y = (-4)^2 + 4(-4) + 1 = 1$ | $(-4, 1)$ |
| 0 | $y = (0)^2 + 4(0) + 1 = 1$ | $(0, 1)$ |

Finally, draw the axis of symmetry, plot the vertex and your table of points, and trace the parabola:

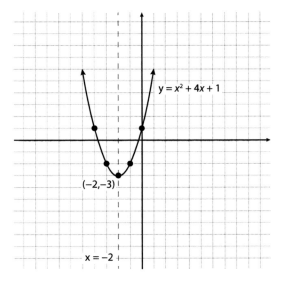

# FUNCTIONS

**Functions** describe how an input relates to an output. Linear equations, sine and cosine are examples of functions. In a function, there must be one and only one output for each input. $\sqrt{x}$ is not a function because there are two outputs for any one input: $\sqrt{4} = 2, -2$.

## Describing Functions

Functions are often written in $f(x)$ form: $f(x) = x^2$ means that for input $x$ the output is $x^2$. In relating functions to linear equations, you can think of $f(x)$ as equivalent to $y$. The **DOMAIN** of a function is all the possible inputs of that function. The **RANGE** of a function includes the outputs of the inputs. For example, for the function $f(x) = x^2$, if the domain includes all positive and negative integers the range will include 0 and only positive integers. When you graph a function, the domain is plotted on the $x$-axis and the range is plotted on the $y$-axis.

## Examples

Given $f(x) = 2x - 10$, find $f(9)$.

Plug in 9 for $x$:

$f(9) = 2(9) - 10$

**$f(9) = 8$**

Given $f(x) = \frac{4}{x}$ with a domain of all positive integers except zero, and $g(x) = \frac{4}{x}$ with a domain of all positive and negative integers except zero, which function has a range that includes the number $-2$?

The function $f(x)$ has a range of only positive numbers, since $x$ cannot be negative. The function $g(x)$ has a range of positive and negative numbers, since $x$ can be either positive or negative. **The number $-2$, therefore, must be in the range for $g(x)$ but not for $f(x)$.**

## Exponential Functions

An **EXPONENTIAL FUNCTION** is in the form $f(x) = a^x$, where $a > 0$. When $a > 1$, $f(x)$ approaches infinity as $x$ increases and zero as $x$ decreases. When $0 < a < 1$, $f(x)$ approaches zero as $x$ increases and infinity as $x$ increases. When $a = 1$, $f(x) = 1$. The graph of an exponential function where $a \neq 1$ will have a horizontal asymptote along the $x$-axis; the graph will never cross below the $x$-axis. The graph of an exponential function where $a = 1$ will be a horizontal line at $y = 1$. All graphs of exponential functions include the points $(0, 1)$ and $(1, a)$.

## Examples

Graph the function $f(x) = 3^x$.

First, estimate the shape and direction of the graph based on the value of $a$. Since $a > 1$, you know that $f(x)$ will approach infinity as $x$ increases and there will be a horizontal asymptote along the negative $x$-axis.

Next, plot the points $(0, 1)$ and $(1, a)$.

Finally, plug in one or two more values for $x$, plot those points and trace the graph:

$f(2) = 3^2 = 9 \rightarrow (2, 9)$

$\longrightarrow$
CONTINUE

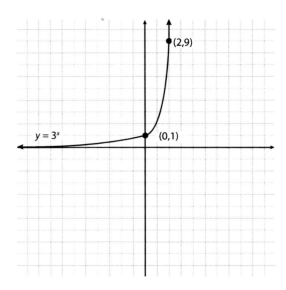

Given $f(x) = 2^x$, solve for $x$ when $f(x) = 64$.

$$64 = 2^x$$

The inverse of an exponent is a log. Take the log of both sides to solve for $x$:

$$\log_2 64 = x$$

$$x = 6$$

## Logarithmic Functions

A **LOGARITHMIC FUNCTION** is the inverse of an exponential function. Remember the definition of a log: if $\log_a x = b$, then $a^b = x$. Logarithmic functions are written in the form $f(x) = \log_a x$, where $a$ is any number greater than 0, except for 1. If $a$ is not shown, it is assumed that $a = 10$. The function $\ln x$ is called a **NATURAL LOG**, equal to $\log_e x$. When $0 < a < 1$, $f(x)$ approaches infinity as $x$ approaches zero and negative infinity as $x$ increases. When $a > 1$, $f(x)$ approaches negative infinity as $x$ approaches zero and infinity as $x$ increases. In either case, the graph of a logarithmic function has a vertical asymptote along the $y$-axis; the graph will never cross to the left of the $y$-axis. All graphs of logarithmic functions include the points $(1, 0)$ and $(a, 1)$.

### Examples

Graph the function $f(x) = \log_4 x$.

First, estimate the shape and direction of the graph based on the value of $a$. Since $a > 1$, you know that $f(x)$ will approach infinity as $x$ increases and there will be a vertical asymptote along the negative $y$-axis.

Next, plot the points $(1, 0)$ and $(a, 1)$.

Finally, it is easier to plug in a value for $f(x)$ and solve for $x$ rather than attempting to solve for $f(x)$. Plug in one or two values for $f(x)$, plot those points and trace the graph:

$$2 = \log_4 x$$

$4^2 = x$

$16 = x \rightarrow (16, 2)$

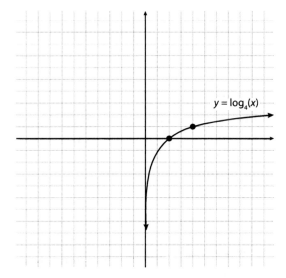

Given $f(x) = \log_{\frac{1}{3}} x$, solve for $f(81)$.

Rewrite the function in exponent form:

$x = \frac{1}{3}^{f(x)}$

$81 = \frac{1}{3}^{f(x)}$

The question is asking: to what power must you raise $\frac{1}{3}$ to get 81?

Recognize that $3^4 = 81$, so $\frac{1}{3}^4 = \frac{1}{81}$

Switch the sign of the exponent to flip the numerator and denominator:

$\frac{1}{3}^{-4} = \frac{81}{1}$

**$f(81) = -4$**

## Arithmetic and Geometric Sequences

SEQUENCES are patterns of numbers. In most questions about sequences you must determine the pattern. In an ARITHMETIC SEQUENCE, add or subtract the same number between terms. In a GEOMETRIC SEQUENCE, multiply or divide by the same number between terms. For example, 2, 6, 10, 14, 18 and 11, 4, –3, –10, –17 are arithmetic sequences because you add 4 to each term in the first example and you subtract 7 from each term in the second example. The sequence 5, 15, 45, 135 is a geometric sequence because you multiply each term by 3. In arithmetic sequences, the number by which you add or subtract is called the COMMON DIFFERENCE. In geometric sequences, the number by which you multiply or divide is called the COMMON RATIO.

In an arithmetic sequence, the $n^{\text{th}}$ term ($a_n$) can be found by calculating $a_n = a_1 + (n - 1)d$, where $d$ is the common difference and $a_1$ is the first term in the sequence. In a geometric sequence, $a_n = a_1(r^n)$, where $r$ is the common ratio.

## Examples

Find the common difference and the next term of the following sequence: 5, −1, −7, −13

> Find the difference between two terms that are next to each other:
>
> $5 − (−1) = −6$
>
> **The common difference is −6.** (It must be negative to show the difference is subtracted, not added.)
>
> Now subtract 6 from the last term to find the next term:
>
> $−13 − 6 = −19$
>
> **The next term is −19.**

Find the 12th term of the following sequence: 2, 6, 18, 54

> First, decide whether this is an arithmetic or geometric sequence. Since the numbers are getting farther and farther apart, you know this must be a geometric sequence.
>
> Divide one term by the term before it to find the common ratio:
>
> $18 ÷ 6 = 3$
>
> Next, plug in the common ratio and the first term to the equation $a_n = a_1(r^n)$:
>
> $a_{12} = 2(3^{12})$
>
> $a_{12} = 1,062,882$
>
> Notice that it would have taken a very long time to multiply each term by 3 until you got the 12th term—this is where that equation comes in handy!

The fourth term of a sequence is 9. The common difference is 11. What is the 10th term?

> To answer this question, you can simply add $9 + 11 = 20$ to get the 5th term, $20 + 11 = 31$ to get the 6th term, and so on until you get the 10th term. Or you can plug the information you know into your equation $a_n = a_1 + (n − 1)d$. In this case, you do not know the first term. If you use the fourth term instead, you must replace $(n − 1)$ with $(n − 4)$:
>
> $a_{10} = 9 + (10 − 4)11$
>
> $a_{10} = 75$

# ABSOLUTE VALUE

The **ABSOLUTE VALUE** of a number (represented by the symbol $|x|$) is its distance from zero, not its value. For example, $|3| = 3$, and $|−3| = 3$ because both 3 and −3 are three units from zero. The absolute value of a number is always positive.

Equations with absolute values will have two answers, so you need to set up two equations. The first is simply the equation with the absolute value symbol removed. For the second equation, isolate the absolute value on one side of the equation and multiply the other side of the equation by −1.

## Examples

Solve for $x$: $|2x - 3| = x + 1$

Set up the first equation by removing the absolute value symbol then solve for $x$:

$|2x - 3| = x + 1$

$2x - 3 = x + 1$

$x = 4$

For the second equation, remove the absolute value and multiply by −1:

$|2x - 3| = x + 1 \rightarrow$

$2x - 3 = -(x + 1) \rightarrow$

$2x - 3 = -x - 1 \rightarrow$

$3x = 2$

$x = \frac{2}{3}$

Both answers are correct, so the complete answer is **$x = 4$ or $\frac{2}{3}$**.

Solve for $y$: $2|y + 4| = 10$

Set up the first equation:

$2(y + 4) = 10$

$y + 4 = 5$

$y = 1$

Set up the second equation. Remember to isolate the absolute value before multiplying by −1:

$2|y + 4| = 10 \rightarrow$

$|y + 4| = 5 \rightarrow$

$y + 4 = -5$

$y = -9$

**$y = 1$ or $-9$**

# SOLVING WORD PROBLEMS

Any of the math concepts discussed here can be turned into a word problem, and you'll likely see word problems in various forms throughout the test. (In fact, you may have noticed that several examples in the ratio and proportion sections were word problems.)

Be sure to read the entire problem before beginning to solve it: a common mistake is to provide an answer to a question that wasn't actually asked. Also, remember that not all of the information provided in a problem is necessarily needed to solve it.

When working multiple-choice word problems like those on the Accuplacer, it's important to check your work. Many of the incorrect

**KEY WORDS**
Word problems generally
contain key words that can
help you determine what math
processes may be required in
order to solve them.
Addition: *added, combined,
increased by, in all, total,
perimeter, sum,* and *more than*
Subtraction: *how much more,
less than, fewer than, exceeds,
difference,* and *decreased*
Multiplication: *of, times, area,*
and *product*
Division: *distribute, share,
average, per, out of, percent,* and
*quotient*
Equals: *is, was, are, amounts to,*
and *were*

answer choices will be those resulting from common mistakes. So even if a solution you calculated is listed as an answer choice, that doesn't necessarily mean you've done the problem correctly—you have to check your own answer to be sure.

## General Steps for Word Problem Solving

Step 1: Read the entire problem and determine what the question is asking.

Step 2: List all of the given data and define the variables.

Step 3: Determine the formula(s) needed or set up equations from the information in the problem.

Step 4: Solve.

Step 5: Check your answer. (Is the amount too large or small? Are the answers in the correct unit of measure?)

## Basic Word Problems

A word problem in algebra is just an equation or a set of equations described using words. Your task when solving these problems is to turn the "story" of the problem into mathematical equations.

### Examples

A store owner bought a case of 48 backpacks for $476.00. He sold 17 of the backpacks in his store for $18 each, and the rest were sold to a school for $15 each. What was the store owner's profit?

Start by listing all the data and defining the variable:

total number of backpacks = 48

cost of backpacks = $476.00

backpacks sold in store at price of $18 = 17

backpacks sold to school at a price of $15 = 75 – 17 = 31

total profit = $x$

Now set up an equation:

*total profit = income – cost* = $(306 + 465) - 476 = 295$

The store owner made a profit of **$295**.

Thirty students in Mr. Joyce's room are working on projects over 2 days. The first day, he gave them $\frac{3}{5}$ hour to work. On the second day, he gave them $\frac{1}{2}$ as much time as the first day. How much time did each student have to work on the project?

Start by listing all the data and defining your variables. Note that the number of students, while given in the problem, is not needed to find the answer:

time on 1st day = $\frac{3}{5}$ hr. = 36 min.

time on 2nd day = $\frac{1}{2}(36)$ = 18 min.

Coverting units can often help
you avoid operations with
fractions when dealing with
time.

total time = $x$

Now set up the equation and solve:

*total time = time on 1st day + time on 2nd day*

$x = 36 + 18 = 54$

The students had **54 minutes** to work on the projects.

## Distance Word Problems

Distance word problems involve something traveling at a constant or average speed. Whenever you read a problem that involves *how fast*, *how far*, or *for how long*, you should think of the distance equation $d = rt$, where $d$ stands for distance, $r$ for rate (speed), and $t$ for time.

These problems can be solved by setting up a grid with $d$, $r$, and $t$ along the top and each moving object on the left. When setting up the grid, make sure the units are consistent. For example, if the distance is in meters and the time is in seconds, the rate should be meters per second.

### Examples

Will drove from his home to the airport at an average speed of 30 mph. He then boarded a helicopter and flew to the hospital at an average speed of 60 mph. The entire distance was 150 miles, and the trip took 3 hours. Find the distance from the airport to the hospital.

The first step is to set up a table and fill in a value for each variable:

|  | $d$ | $r$ | $t$ |
|---|---|---|---|
| driving | $d$ | 30 | $t$ |
| flying | $150 - d$ | 60 | $3 - t$ |

You can now set up equations for driving and flying. The first row gives the equation $d = 30t$ and the second row gives the equation $150 - d = 60(3 - t)$.

Next, solve this system of equations. Start by substituting for $d$ in the second equation:

$d = 30t$

$150 - d = 60(30 - t) \rightarrow 150 - 30t = 60(30 - t)$

Now solve for $t$:

$150 - 30t = 180 - 60t$

$-30 = -30t$

$1 = t$

Although you've solved for $t$, you're not done yet. Notice that the problem asks for distance. So, you need to solve for $d$: what the problem asked for. It does not ask for time, but you need to calculate it to solve the problem.

Driving: $30t = 30$ miles

Flying: $150 - d = 120$ miles

The distance from the airport to the hospital is **120 miles**.

Two riders on horseback start at the same time from opposite ends of a field that is 45 miles long. One horse is moving at 14 mph and the second horse is moving at 16 mph. How long after they begin will they meet?

First, set up the table. The variable for time will be the same for each, because they will have been on the field for the same amount of time when they meet:

|  | $d$ | $r$ | $t$ |
| --- | --- | --- | --- |
| horse #1 | $d$ | 14 | $t$ |
| horse #2 | $45 - d$ | 16 | $t$ |

Next set up two equations:

Horse #1: $d = 14t$

Horse #2: $45 - d = 16t$

Now substitute and solve:

$d = 14t$

$45 - d = 16t \rightarrow 45 - 14t = 16t$

$45 = 30t$

$t = 1.5$

They will meet **1.5 hr.** after they begin.

The Accuplacer will give you most of the formulas you need to work problems, but they won't give you the formulas for percent change or work problems.

## Work Problems

WORK PROBLEMS involve situations where several people or machines are doing work at different rates. Your task is usually to figure out how long it will take these people or machines to complete a task while working together. The trick to doing work problems is to figure out how much of the project each person or machine completes in the same unit of time. For example, you might calculate how much of a wall a person can paint in 1 hour, or how many boxes an assembly line can pack in 1 minute.

The next step is to set up an equation to solve for the total time. This equation is usually similar to the equation for distance, but here *work = rate × time*.

See *Adding and Subtracting Fractions* for step-by-step instruction on operations with fractions.

### Examples

Bridget can clean an entire house in 12 hours while her brother Tom takes 8 hours. How long would it take for Bridget and Tom to clean 2 houses together?

Start by figuring out how much of a house each sibling can clean on his or her own. Bridget can clean the house in 12 hours, so she can clean $\frac{1}{12}$ of the house in an hour. Using the same logic, Tom can clean $\frac{1}{8}$ of a house in an hour.

By adding these values together, you get the fraction of the house they can clean together in an hour :

$\frac{1}{12} + \frac{1}{8} = \frac{5}{24}$

They can do $\frac{5}{24}$ of the job per hour.

Now set up variables and an equation to solve:

$t$ = time spent cleaning (in hours)

$h$ = number of houses cleaned = 2

$work = rate \times time$

$h = \frac{5}{24}t \rightarrow$

$2 = \frac{5}{24}t \rightarrow$

$t = \frac{48}{5} = \mathbf{9\frac{3}{5}}$ **hr.**

Farmer Dan needs to water his cornfield. One hose can water a field 1.25 times faster than a second hose. When both hoses are running, they water the field together in 5 hours. How long would it take to water the field if only the slower hose is used?

In this problem you don't know the exact time, but you can still find the hourly rate as a variable:

The second hose completes the job in $f$ hours, so it waters $\frac{1}{f}$ field per hour. The faster hose waters the field in 1.25$f$, so it waters the field in $\frac{1}{1.25f}$ hours. Together, they take 5 hours to water the field, so they water $\frac{1}{5}$ of the field per hour.

Now you can set up the equations and solve:

$\frac{1}{f} + \frac{1}{1.25f} = \frac{1}{5} \rightarrow$

$1.25f\left(\frac{1}{f} + \frac{1}{1.25f}\right) = 1.25f\left(\frac{1}{5}\right) \rightarrow$

$1.25 + 1 = 0.25f$

$2.25 = 0.25f$

$f = 9$

The fast hose takes 9 hours to water the field. The slow hose takes 1.25(9) = **11.25 hours**.

Martha takes 2 hours to pick 500 apples, and George takes 3 hours to pick 450 apples. How long will they take, working together, to pick 1000 apples?

Calculate how many apples each person can pick per hour:

Martha: $\frac{500 \text{ apples}}{2 \text{ hrs}} = \frac{250 \text{ apples}}{\text{hr}}$

George: $\frac{450 \text{ apples}}{3 \text{ hrs}} = \frac{150 \text{ apples}}{\text{hr}}$

Together: $\frac{(250 + 150)\text{apples}}{\text{hr}} = \frac{400 \text{ apples}}{\text{hr}}$

Now set up an equation to find the time it takes to pick 1000 apples:

total time $= \frac{1 \text{ hr}}{400 \text{ apples}} \times 1000 \text{ apples} = \frac{1000}{400}$ hrs = **2.5 hrs**

$\longrightarrow$

CONTINUE

# 3

# GEOMETRY

O n the ACCUPLACER, geometry and trigonometry appear mainly on the College-Level Math test, but it is a good idea for all students to review these subjects. Geometry may appear in questions on the Arithmetic test as part of applying arithmetic concepts. Expect the College-Level Math test to cover coordinate geometry, and logarithmic and trigonometric functions.

## PROPERTIES OF SHAPES

### Area and Perimeter

AREA and PERIMETER problems require you to use the equations shown in the table below to find either the area inside a shape or the distance around it (the perimeter). These equations will not be given on the test, so you need to have them memorized on test day.

These equations aren't given to you on test day—you need to have them memorized.

Table 3.1. Area and Perimeter

| SHAPE | AREA | PERIMETER |
|---|---|---|
| CIRCLE | $A = \pi r^2$ | $C = 2\pi r = \pi d$ |
| TRIANGLE | $A = \dfrac{b \times h}{2}$ | $P = s_1 + s_2 + s_3$ |
| SQUARE | $A = s^2$ | $P = 4s$ |
| RECTANGLE | $A = l \times w$ | $P = 2l + 2w$ |

### Examples

A farmer has purchased 100 meters of fencing to enclose his rectangular garden. If one side of the garden is 20 meters long and the other is 28 meters long, how much fencing will the farmer have left over?

The perimeter of a rectangle is equal to twice its length plus twice its width:

$P = 2(20) + 2(28) = 96 \text{ m}$

The farmer has 100 meters of fencing, so he'll have 100 − 96 = **4 meters** left.

Taylor is going to paint a square wall that is 3.5 meters high. How much paint will he need?

Each side of the square wall is 3.5 meters:

$A = 3.5^2 = $ **12.25 m**

## Volume

**VOLUME** is the amount of space taken up by a three-dimensional object. Different formulas are used to find the volumes of different shapes.

Table 3.2. Volume

| SHAPE | VOLUME |
| --- | --- |
| CYLINDER | $V = \pi r^2 h$ |
| PYRAMID | $V = \frac{l \times w \times h}{3}$ |
| CONE | $V = \pi r^2 \frac{h}{3}$ |
| SPHERE | $V = \frac{4}{3}\pi r^3$ |

### Examples

Charlotte wants to fill her circular swimming pool with water. The pool has a diameter of 6 meters and is 1 meter deep. How many cubic meters of water will she need to fill the pool?

This question is asking about the volume of Charlotte's pool. The circular pool is actually a cylinder, so use the formula for a cylinder: $V = \pi r^2 h$.

The diameter is 6 meters. The radius is half the diameter so $r = 6 \div 2 = 3$ meters.

Now solve for the volume:

$V = \pi r^2 h$

$V = \pi(3 \text{ m})^2(1 \text{ m})$

$V = 28.3 \text{ m}^3$

**Charlotte will need approximately 28.3 cubic meters of water to fill her pool.**

Danny has a fishbowl that is filled to the brim with water and purchased some spherical glass marbles to line the bottom of it. He dropped in four marbles, and water spilled out of the fishbowl. If the radius of each marble is 1 centimeter, how much water spilled?

Since the fishbowl was filled to the brim, the volume of the water that spilled out of It is equal to the volume of the marbles that Danny dropped into it. First, find the volume of one marble using the equation for a sphere:

$V = \frac{4}{3}\pi r^3$

$$V = \frac{4}{3}\pi(1 \text{ cm})^3$$

$$V = 4.2 \text{ cm}^3$$

Since Danny dropped in 4 marbles, multiply this volume by 4 to find the total volume:

$$4.2 \text{ cm}^3 \times 4 = 16.8 \text{ cm}^3$$

**Approximately 16.8 cubic centimeters of water spilled out of the fishbowl.**

### Circles

The definition of a circle is the set of points that are equal distance from a center point. The distance from the center to any given point on the circle is the RADIUS. If you draw a straight line segment across the circle going through the center, the distance along the line segment from one side of the circle to the other is called the diameter. The radius is always equal to half the diameter:

$$d = 2r$$

A CENTRAL ANGLE is formed by drawing radii out from the center to two points $A$ and $B$ along the circle. The INTERCEPTED ARC is the portion of the circle (the arc length) between points $A$ and $B$. You can find the intercepted arc length $l$ if you know the central angle $\theta$ and vice versa:

$$l = 2\pi r \frac{\theta}{360°}$$

A CHORD is a line segment that connects two points on a circle. Unlike the diameter, a chord does not have to go through the center. You can find the chord length if you know either the central angle $\theta$ or the radius of the circle $r$ and the distance from the center of the circle to the chord $d$ ($d$ must be at a right angle to the chord):

If you know the central angle, chord length = $2r\sin\frac{\theta}{2}$

If you know the radius and distance, chord length = $2\sqrt{r^2 - d^2}$

A SECANT is similar to a chord; it connects two points on a circle. The difference is that a secant is a line, not a line segment, so it extends outside of the circle on either side.

A TANGENT is a straight line that touches a circle at only one point.

A SECTOR is the area within a circle that is enclosed by a central angle; if a circle is a pie, a sector is the piece of pie cut by two radii. You can find the AREA OF A SECTOR if you know either the central angle $\theta$ or the arc length $l$.

If you know the central angle, the area of the sector = $\pi r^2 \frac{\theta}{360°}$

If you know the arc length, the area of a sector = $\frac{1}{2}rl$

There are two other types of angles you can create in or around a circle. INSCRIBED ANGLES are <u>inside</u> the circle: the vertex is a point $P$ on the circle and the rays extend to two other points on the circle

(*A* and *B*). As long as *A* and *B* remain constant, you can move the vertex *P* anywhere along the circle and the inscribed angle will be the same. **CIRCUMSCRIBED ANGLES** are <u>outside</u> of the circle: the rays are formed by two tangent lines that touch the circle at points *A* and *B*.

You can find the inscribed angle if you know the radius of the circle r and the arc length *l* between *A* and *B*:

inscribed angle $= \frac{90°l}{\pi r}$

To find the circumscribed angle, find the central angle formed by the same points *A* and *B* and subtract that angle from 180°.

## Examples

A circle has a diameter of 10 centimeters. What is the intercepted arc length between points *A* and *B* if the central angle between those points measures 46°?

First divide the diameter by two to find the radius:

$r = 10 \text{ cm} \div 2 = 5 \text{ cm}$

Now use the formula for intercepted arc length:

$l = 2\pi r \frac{\theta}{360°}$

$l = 2\pi (5 \text{ cm}) \frac{46°}{360°}$

**$l = 4.0 \text{ cm}$**

A chord is formed by line segment $\overline{QP}$. The radius of the circle is
5 cm and the chord length is 6 cm. Find the distance from center *C* to the chord.

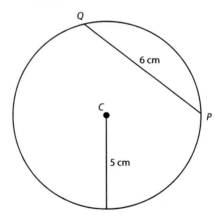

Use the formula for chord length:

chord length $= 2\sqrt{r^2 - d^2}$

In this example, we are told the chord length and the radius, and we need to solve for d:

$6 \text{ cm} = 2R(5 \text{ cm})^2 - d^2$

$3 \text{ cm} = R(5 \text{ cm})^2 - d^2$

$9 \text{ cm}^2 = 25 \text{ cm}^2 - d^2$

$d^2 = 16 \text{ cm}^2$

**$d = 4 \text{ cm}$**

Points *A* and *B* are located on a circle. The arc length between *A* and *B* is 2 centimeters. The diameter of the circle is 8 centimeters. Find the inscribed angle.

First, divide the diameter by two to find the radius:

$r = \frac{1}{2}(8 \text{ cm})$

$r = 4 \text{ cm}$

Now use the formula for an inscribed angle:

inscribed angle $= \frac{90°l}{\pi r}$

inscribed angle $= \frac{90°(2 \text{ cm})}{\pi(4 \text{ cm})}$

**inscribed angle = 14.3°**

## CONGRUENCE

CONGRUENCE means having the same size and shape. Two shapes are congruent if you can turn (rotate), flip (reflect), and/or slide (translate) one to fit perfectly on top of the other. Two angles are congruent if they measure the same number of degrees; they do not have to face the same direction nor must they necessarily have rays of equal length.

If two triangles have one of the combinations of congruent sides and/or angles listed below, then those triangles are congruent:

**SSS** – *side, side, side*

**ASA** – *angle, side, angle*

**SAS** – *side, angle, side*

**AAS** – *angle, angle, side*

An ISOSCELES TRIANGLE has two sides of equal length. The sides of equal length are called the legs and the third side is called the base. If you bisect an isosceles triangle by drawing a line perpendicular to the base, you will form two congruent right triangles.

Where two lines cross and form an X, the opposite angles are congruent and are called VERTICAL ANGLES.

PARALLEL LINES are lines that never cross. If you cut two parallel lines by a transversal, you will form four pairs of congruent COR-RESPONDING ANGLES.

A PARALLELOGRAM is a quadrilateral in which both pairs of opposite sides are parallel and congruent (of equal length). In a parallelogram, the two pairs of opposite angles are also congruent. If you divide a parallelogram by either of the diagonals, you will form two congruent triangles.

CONTINUE

## Examples

Kate and Emily set out for a bike ride together from their house. They ride 6 miles north, then Kate turns 30° to the west and Emily turns 30° to the east. They both ride another 8 miles. If Kate rides 12 miles to return home, how far must Emily ride to get home?

> Draw out Kate's and Emily's trips to see that they form triangles. The triangles have corresponding sides with lengths of 6 miles and 8 miles, and a corresponding angle in between of 120°. This fits the "SAS" rule so the triangles must be congruent. The length Kate has to ride home corresponds to the length Emily has to ride home, so **Emily must ride 12 miles**.

Angle A measures 53°. Find angle H.

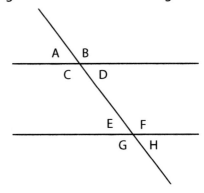

> For parallel lines cut by a transversal, look for vertical and corresponding angles.
>
> Angles *A* and *D* are vertical angles, so angle *D* must be congruent to angle *A*. Angle *D* = 53°.
>
> Angles *D* and *H* are corresponding angles, so angle *H* must be congruent to angle *D*. **Angle *H* = 53°**.

# RIGHT TRIANGLES AND TRIGONOMETRY

## Pythagorean Theorem

Shapes with 3 sides are known as TRIANGLES. In addition to knowing the formulas for their area and perimeter, you should also know the Pythagorean Theorem, which describes the relationship between the three sides (*a*, *b*, and *c*) of a triangle:

$$a^2 + b^2 = c^2$$

## Example

Erica is going to run a race in which she'll run 3 miles due north and 4 miles due east. She'll then run back to the starting line. How far will she run during this race?

> Start by drawing a picture of Erica's route. You'll see it forms a triangle:

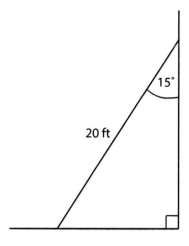

One leg of the triangle is missing, but you can find its length using the Pythagorean Theorem:

$a^2 + b^2 = c^2$

$3^2 + 4^2 = c^2$

$25 = c{\_}{\char`\^}2$

$c = 5$

Adding all 3 sides gives the length of the whole race:

$3 + 4 + 5 = $ **12 mi**

## Trigonometry

Using **TRIGONOMETRY**, you can calculate an angle in a right triangle based on the ratio of two sides of that triangle. You can also calculate one of the side lengths using the measure of an angle and another side. **SINE (SIN)**, **COSINE (COS)**, and **TANGENT (TAN)** correspond to the three possible ratios of side lengths. They are defined below:

*sin 0 = opposite/hypotenuse*

*cos 0 = adjacent/hypotenuse*

*tan 0 = opposite/adjacent*

*Opposite* is the side opposite from the angle 0, *adjacent* is the side adjacent to the angle 0, and *hypotenuse* is the longest side of the triangle, opposite from the right angle. SOH-CAH-TOA is an acronym to help you remember which ratio goes with which function.

When solving for a side or an angle in a right triangle, first identify which function to use based on the known lengths or angle.

### Examples

Phil is hanging holiday lights. To do so safely, he must lean his 20-foot ladder against the outside of his house an angle of 15° or less. How far from the house he can safely place the base of the ladder?

Draw a triangle with the known length and angle labeled.

The known side (the length of the ladder) is the

hypotenuse of the triangle, and the unknown distance is the side opposite the angle. Therefore, you can use sine:

$$\sin\theta = \frac{opposite}{hypotenuse}$$

$$\sin 15° = \frac{opposite}{20\ feet}$$

Now solve for the opposite side:

$$opposite = \sin 15°(20\ feet)$$

**opposite = 5.2 feet**

Grace is practicing shooting hoops. She is 5 feet 4 inches tall; her basketball hoop is 10 feet high. From 8 feet away, at what angle does she have to look up to see the hoop? Assume that her eyes are 4 inches lower than the top of her head.

Draw a diagram and notice that the line from Grace's eyes to the hoop of the basket forms the hypotenuse of a right triangle. The side adjacent to the angle of her eyes is the distance from the basket: 8 feet. The side opposite to Grace's eyes is the difference between the height of her eyes and the height of the basket: 10 feet − 5 feet = 5 feet.

Next, use the formula for tangent to solve for the angle:

$$\tan\theta = \frac{opposite}{adjacent}$$

$$\tan\theta = \frac{5\ ft}{8\ ft}$$

Now take the inverse tangent of both sides to solve for the angle:

$$\theta = \tan^{-1}\frac{5}{8}$$

**θ = 32°**

## COORDINATE GEOMETRY

Coordinate geometry is the study of points, lines, and shapes that have been graphed on a set of axes.

### Points, Lines, and Planes

In coordinate geometry, points are plotted on a **COORDINATE PLANE**, a two-dimensional plane in which the *x*-**AXIS** indicates horizontal direction and the *y*-**AXIS** indicates vertical direction. The intersection of these two axes is the origin. Points are defined by their location in relation to the horizontal and vertical axes. The coordinates of a point are written $(x, y)$. The coordinates of the origin are $(0, 0)$. The *x* coordinates to the right of the origin and the *y*-coordinates above it are positive; the *x*-coordinates to the left of the origin and the *y*-coordinates below it are negative.

A line is formed by connecting any two points on a coordinate plane; lines are continuous in both directions. Lines can be defined by their slope, or steepness, and their *y*-**INTERCEPT**, or the point at which they intersect the *y*-axis. A line is represented by the equation $y = mx + b$. The constant *m* represents slope and the constant *b* represents the *y*-intercept.

## Examples

Matt parks his car near a forest where he goes hiking. From his car he hikes 1 mile north, 2 miles east, then 3 miles west. If his car represents the origin, find the coordinates of Matt's current location.

To find the coordinates, you must find Matt's displacement along the x- and y-axes. Matt hiked 1 mile north and zero miles south, so his displacement along the y-axis is +1 mile. Matt hiked 2 miles east and 3 miles west, so his displacement along the x axis is +2 miles − 3 miles = −1 mile.

**Matt's coordinates are (−1, 1).**

A square is drawn on a coordinate plane. The bottom corners are located at (−2, 3) and (4, 3). What are the coordinates for the top right corner?

Draw the coordinate plane and plot the given points. If you connect these points you will see that the bottom side is 6 units long. Since it is a square, all sides must be 6 units long. Count 6 units up from the point (4, 3) to find the top right corner.

**The coordinates for the top right corner are (4, 9).**

## The Distance and Midpoint Formulas

To determine the distance between the points $(x_1, y_1)$ and $(x_2, y_2)$ from a grid use the formula $d = \sqrt{(x_2 - x_1)^2 + (y_2 - y_1)^2}$. The midpoint, which is halfway between the 2 points, is the point $\left(\frac{x_1 + x_2}{2}, \frac{y_1 + y_2}{2}\right)$.

## Examples

What is the distance between points (3, −6) and (−5, 2)?

Plug the values for $x_1$, $x_2$, $y_1$, and $y_2$ into the distance formula and simplify:

$$d = \sqrt{(-5 - 3)^2 + (2 - (-6))^2} = \sqrt{64 + 64} = \sqrt{64 \times 2} = 8\sqrt{2}$$

What is the midpoint between points (3, −6) and (−5, 2)?

Plug the values for $x_1$, $x_2$, $y_1$, and $y_2$ into the midpoint formula and simplify:

$$\text{midpoint} = \left(\frac{3 + (-5)}{2}, \frac{(-6) + 2}{2}\right) = \left(\frac{-2}{2}, \frac{-4}{2}\right) = (-1, -2)$$

# PART II: READING

The ACCUPLACER contains three reading tests: Reading Comprehension, ESL – Reading Skills, and ESL – Sentence Meaning.

There are two types of questions on the Reading Comprehension test: passage-based and sentence relationships. Passage-based questions consist of one passage followed by a question. The passage may be fifty to two hundred words long; questions may ask you to identify the main idea of a passage or its purpose, to identify supporting details or evidence for the writer's argument, or to draw conclusions or identify implications from the text. Sentence relationship questions present two related sentences followed by a question that will ask you to explain how the second sentence relates to the first. Questions may ask if the second sentence expands on the first, presents a contradiction, presents a contrast, or draws a conclusion.

The ESL – Reading Skills test focuses on comprehension of short passages. Passages are fifty to ninety words long and followed by questions asking you to identify the main idea of a passage or its purpose, to identify supporting details or evidence for the writer's argument, or to draw conclusions or identify implications from the text. Other questions on this test will ask you to explain vocabulary or phrasing, paraphrase the passage, or locate pertinent information.

The ESL – Sentence Meaning test focuses on comprehension of sentences. You will be asked what words or phrases mean in context, or how to best paraphrase the sentence.

# 4

# READING

The ACCUPLCER Reading section assesses your ability to summarize, interpret, and draw conclusions about both non-fiction and fiction passages. On the test, you will read both types of passages; specific questions may ask about the following:

- the main idea of a passage
- the role of supporting details in a passage
- adding supporting details to a passage
- the structure of a passage
- the author's purpose
- logical inferences that can be drawn from a passage
- comparing passages
- vocabulary and figurative language

The questions more broadly fall under four general question types:

**MAIN IDEA:** A question may directly or indirectly ask you about the main idea of a passage. Summarizing it briefly in your own words or reviewing the first few paragraphs will help you identify the main idea and narrow down your answer choices.

**ABOUT THE AUTHOR:** These questions ask about the author's attitude, thoughts, and opinions. To determine the correct response, pay attention to context clues in the text. The answer may not be explicitly stated but instead conveyed in the overall message.

**PASSAGE FACTS:** To answer these questions correctly,

you must distinguish between facts and opinions presented in the passage. You may also be asked to identify specific information provided by the author.

ADDITIONAL INFORMATION: These questions ask you to consider what information could be added to or was missing from the passage; they may even provide a fill-in-the-blank option to include a new statement at a certain point in the text. Keep in mind that any additional information should strengthen the author's argument. These questions may also ask in what direction the passage was going; that is, about logical inferences that can be drawn from the text.

## STRATEGIES

Despite the different types of questions you will face, there are some strategies for Reading Comprehension that always apply:

- Read the questions before reading the passage. You will save time, as you will know what to look out for as you read.

- Use the process of elimination. Often at least one answer choice in a question is obviously incorrect. After reading the passage, eliminate any blatantly incorrect answer choices to increase your chances of finding the correct answer much more quickly.

- Avoid negative statements. Correct responses tend to be neutral or positive, so if it seems like an answer choice has a negative connotation, it is very likely that the answer is intentionally false.

## THE MAIN IDEA

The main idea of a text is the author's purpose in writing a book, article, story, etc. Being able to identify and understand the main idea is a critical skill necessary to comprehend and appreciate what you're reading.

Consider a political election. A candidate is running for office and plans to deliver a speech asserting her position on tax reform. The topic of the speech—tax reform—is clear to voters, and probably of interest to many. However, imagine that the candidate believes that taxes should be lowered. She is likely to assert this argument in her speech, supporting it with examples proving why lowering taxes would benefit the public and how it could be accomplished. While the topic of the speech would be tax reform, the benefit of lowering taxes would be the main idea. Other candidates may have different perspectives on the topic; they may believe that higher taxes are necessary, or that current taxes are adequate. It is likely that their speeches, while on the same topic of tax reform, would have different main ideas: different arguments likewise supported by different examples. Determining what a speaker, writer, or text is asserting about a specific issue will reveal the main idea.

One more quick note: the exam may also ask about a passage's theme, which is similar to but distinct from its topic. While a topic is usually a specific person, place, thing, or issue, the theme is an idea or concept that the author refers back to frequently. Examples of common themes include ideas like the importance of family, the dangers of technology, and the beauty of nature.

There will be many questions on the exam that require you to differentiate between the topic, theme, and main idea of a passage. Let's look at an example:

> Babe Didrikson Zaharias, one of the most decorated female athletes of the twentieth century, is an inspiration for everyone. Born in 1911 in Beaumont, Texas, Zaharias lived in a time when women were considered second-class to men, but she never let that stop her from becoming a champion. Babe was one of seven children in a poor immigrant family, and was competitive from an early age. As a child she excelled at most things she tried, especially sports, which continued into high school and beyond. After high school, Babe played amateur basketball for two years, and soon after began training in track and field. Despite the fact that women were only allowed to enter in three events, Babe represented the United States in the 1932 Los Angeles Olympics, and won two gold medals and one silver for track and field events.
>
> In the early 1930s, Babe began playing golf which earned her a legacy. The first tournament she entered was a men's only tournament; however she did not make the cut to play. Playing golf as an amateur was the only option for a woman at this time, since there was no professional women's league. Babe played as an amateur for a little over a decade, until she turned pro in 1947 for the Ladies Professional Golf Association (LPGA) of which she was a founding member. During her career as a golfer, Babe won eighty-two tournaments, amateur and professional, including the U.S. Women's Open, All-American Open, and British Women's Open Golf Tournament. In 1953, Babe was diagnosed with cancer, but fourteen weeks later, she played

in a tournament. That year she won her third U.S. Women's Open. However by 1955, she didn't have the physicality to compete anymore, and she died of the disease in 1956.

The topic of this passage is obviously Babe Zaharias—the whole passage describes events from her life. Determining the main idea, however, requires a little more analysis. The passage describes Babe Zaharias' life, but the main idea of the paragraph is what it says *about* her life. To figure out the main idea, consider what the writer is saying about Babe Zaharias. The writer is saying that she's someone to admire—that's the main idea and what unites all the information in the paragraph. Lastly, what might the theme of the passage be? The writer refers to several broad concepts, including never giving up and overcoming the odds, both of which could be themes for the passage. Two major indicators of the main idea of a paragraph or passage follow below:

- It is a general idea; it applies to all the more specific ideas in the passage. Every other sentence in a paragraph should be able to relate in some way to the main idea.

- It asserts a specific viewpoint that the author supports with facts, opinions, or other details. In other words, the main idea takes a stand.

## Example

From so far away it's easy to imagine the surface of our solar system's planets as enigmas—how could we ever know what those far-flung planets really look like? It turns out, however, that scientists have a number of tools at their disposal that allow them to paint detailed pictures of many planets' surfaces. The topography of Venus, for example, has been explored by several space probes, including the Russian Venera landers and NASA's Magellan orbiter. These craft used imaging and radar to map the surface of the planet, identifying a whole host of features including volcanoes, craters, and a complex system of channels. Mars has similarly been mapped by space probes, including the famous Mars Rovers, which are automated vehicles that actually landed on the surface of Mars. These rovers have been used by NASA and other space agencies to study the geology, climate, and possible biology of the planet.

In addition these long-range probes, NASA has also used its series of orbiting telescopes to study distant planets. These four massively powerful telescopes include the famous Hubble Space Telescope as well as the Compton Gamma Ray Observatory, Chandra X-Ray Observatory, and the Spitzer Space Telescope. Scientists can use these telescopes to examine planets using not only visible light but also infrared and near-infrared light, ultraviolet light, x-rays and gamma rays.

Powerful telescopes aren't just found in space: NASA makes

use of Earth-bound telescopes as well. Scientists at the National Radio Astronomy Observatory in Charlottesville, VA, have spent decades using radio imaging to build an incredibly detailed portrait of Venus' surface. In fact, Earth-bound telescopes offer a distinct advantage over orbiting telescopes because they allow scientists to capture data from a fixed point, which in turn allows them to effectively compare data collected over long period of time.

Which of the following sentences best describes the main idea of the passage?

**A)** It's impossible to know what the surfaces of other planets are really like.

**B)** Telescopes are an important tool for scientists studying planets in our solar system.

**C)** Venus' surface has many of the same features as the Earth's, including volcanoes, craters, and channels.

**D)** Scientists use a variety of advanced technologies to study the surface of the planets in our solar system.

Answer A) can be eliminated because it directly contradicts the rest of the passage. Answers B) and C) can also be eliminated because they offer only specific details from the passage—while both choices contain details from the passage, neither is general enough to encompass the passage as a whole. **Only answer D) provides an assertion that is both backed up by the passage's content and general enough to cover the entire passage.**

## Topic and Summary Sentences

The main idea of a paragraph usually appears within the TOPIC SENTENCE. The topic sentence introduces the main idea to readers; it indicates not only the topic of a passage, but also the writer's perspective on the topic. Notice, for example, how the first sentence in the example paragraph about Babe Zaharias states the main idea: *Babe Didrikson Zaharias, one of the most decorated female athletes of the twentieth century, is an inspiration for everyone.*

Even though paragraphs generally begin with topic sentences due to their introductory nature, on occasion writers build up to the topic sentence by using supporting details in order to generate interest or build an argument. Be alert for paragraphs when writers do not include a clear topic sentence at all; even without a clear topic sentence, a paragraph will still have a main idea. You may also see a SUMMARY SENTENCE at the end of a passage. As its name suggests, this sentence sums up the passage, often by restating the main idea and the author's key evidence supporting it.

### Example

*In the following paragraph, what are the topic and summary sentences?*

The Constitution of the United States establishes a series

of limits to rein in centralized power. Separation of powers distributes federal authority among three competing branches: the executive, the legislative, and the judicial. Checks and balances allow the branches to check the usurpation of power by any one branch. States' rights are protected under the Constitution from too much encroachment by the federal government. Enumeration of powers names the specific and few powers the federal government has. These four restrictions have helped sustain the American republic for over two centuries.

**The topic sentence is the first sentence in the paragraph.** It introduces the topic of discussion, in this case the constitutional limits aimed at resisting centralized power. **The summary sentence is the last sentence in the paragraph.** It sums up the information that was just presented: here, that constitutional limits have helped sustain the United States of America for over two hundred years.

### Implied Main Idea

A paragraph without a clear topic sentence still has a main idea; rather than clearly stated, it is implied. Determining the IMPLIED MAIN IDEA requires some detective work: you will need to look at the author's word choice and tone in addition to the content of the passage to find his or her main idea. Let's look at an example paragraph.

#### Examples

One of my summer reading books was *Mockingjay*. Though it's several hundred pages long, I read it in just a few days. I was captivated by the adventures of the main character and the complicated plot of the book. However, I felt like the ending didn't reflect the excitement of the story. Given what a powerful personality the main character has, I felt like the ending didn't do her justice.

Even without a clear topic sentence, this paragraph has a main idea. What is the writer's perspective on the book—what is the writer saying about it?

**A)** *Mockingjay* is a terrific novel.

**B)** *Mockingjay* is disappointing.

**C)** *Mockingjay* is full of suspense.

**D)** *Mockingjay* is a lousy novel.

**The correct answer is B): the novel is disappointing.** The process of elimination will reveal the correct answer if that is not immediately clear. While that the paragraph begins with positive commentary on the book—I was captivated by the adventures of the main character and the complicated plot of the book—this positive idea is followed by the contradictory transition word however. A) cannot be the correct answer because the author concludes that the novel was poor. Likewise, D) cannot be correct because it does not encompass all the ideas in the paragraph; despite the negative conclusion,

Understanding the tone of a passage can help you quickly eliminate answer choices.

the author enjoyed most of the book. The main idea should be able to encompass all of the thoughts in a paragraph; choice D) does not apply to the beginning of this paragraph. Finally, choice C) is too specific; it could only apply to the brief description of the plot and adventures of the main character. That leaves choice B) as the best option. The author initially enjoyed the book, but was disappointed by the ending, which seemed unworthy of the exciting plot and character.

Fortunately, none of Alyssa's coworkers has ever seen inside the large filing drawer in her desk. Disguised by the meticulous neatness of the rest of her workspace, there was no sign of the chaos beneath. To even open it, she had to struggle for several minutes with the enormous pile of junk jamming the drawer, until it would suddenly give way, and papers, folders, and candy wrappers spilled out of the top and onto the floor. It was an organizational nightmare, with torn notes and spreadsheets haphazardly thrown on top of each other, and melted candy smeared across pages. She was worried the odor would soon permeate to her coworker's desks, revealing to them her secret.

Which of the following expresses the main idea of this paragraph?

**A)** Alyssa wishes she could move to a new desk.

**B)** Alyssa wishes she had her own office.

**C)** Alyssa is glad none of her coworkers know about her messy drawer.

**D)** Alyssa is sad because she doesn't have any coworkers.

**What the paragraph adds up to is that Alyssa is terribly embarrassed about her messy drawer, and she's glad that none of her coworkers have seen it, making C) the correct answer choice.** This is the main idea. The paragraph opens with the word *fortunately*, so we know that she thinks it's a good thing that none of her coworkers have seen inside the drawer. Plus, notice how the drawer is described: *it was an organizational nightmare*, and it apparently doesn't even function properly: *to even open the drawer, she had to struggle for several minutes.* The writer reveals that it has an odor, with *melted candy* inside. Alyssa is clearly ashamed of her drawer and worries about what her coworkers would think if they saw inside it.

# SUPPORTING DETAILS

SUPPORTING DETAILS provide more support for the author's main idea. For instance, in the Babe Zaharias example, the writer makes the general assertion that *Babe Didrikson Zaharias, one of the most decorated female athletes of the twentieth century, is an inspiration for everyone.* The other sentences offer specific facts and details that prove why she is an inspiration: the names of the illnesses she overcame, and the specific years she competed in the Olympics.

**SIGNAL WORDS**
- For example
- Specifically
- In addition
- Furthermore
- For instance
- Others
- In particular
- Some

Writers often provide clues that can help you identify supporting details. These SIGNAL WORDS tell you that a supporting fact or idea will follow, and so can be helpful in identifying supporting details. Signal words can also help you rule out sentences that are not the main idea or topic sentence: if a sentence begins with one of these phrases, it will likely be too specific to be a main idea.

## Examples

From so far away it's easy to imagine the surface of our solar system's planets as enigmas—how could we ever know what those far-flung planets really look like? It turns out, however, that scientists have a number of tools at their disposal that allow them to paint detailed pictures of many planets' surfaces. The topography of Venus, for example, has been explored by several space probes, including the Russian Venera landers and NASA's Magellan orbiter. These craft used imaging and radar to map the surface of the planet, identifying a whole host of features including volcanoes, craters, and a complex system of channels. Mars has similarly been mapped by space probes, including the famous Mars Rovers, which are automated vehicles that actually landed on the surface of Mars. These rovers have been used by NASA and other space agencies to study the geology, climate, and possible biology of the planet.

In addition to these long-range probes, NASA has also used its series of orbiting telescopes to study distant planets. These four massively powerful telescopes include the famous Hubble Space Telescope as well as the Compton Gamma Ray Observatory, Chandra X-Ray Observatory, and the Spitzer Space Telescope. Scientists can use these telescopes to examine planets using not only visible light but also infrared and near-infrared light, ultraviolet light, x-rays and gamma rays.

Powerful telescopes aren't just found in space: NASA makes use of Earth-bound telescopes as well. Scientists at the National Radio Astronomy Observatory in Charlottesville, VA, have spent decades using radio imaging to build an incredibly detailed portrait of Venus' surface. In fact, Earth-bound telescopes offer a distinct advantage over orbiting telescopes because they allow scientists to capture data from a fixed point, which in turn allows them to effectively compare data collected over long period of time.

1. Which sentence from the text best helps develop the idea that scientists make use of many different technologies to study the surfaces of other planets?

   A) These rovers have been used by NASA and other space agencies to study the geology, climate, and possible biology of the planet.

   B) From so far away it's easy to imagine the surface of our solar system's planets as enigmas—how could we ever know what those far-flung planets really look like?

   C) In addition these long-range probes, NASA has also used its series of orbiting telescopes to study distant planets.

   D) These craft used imaging and radar to map the surface of the planet, identifying a whole host of features including volcanoes, craters, and a complex system of channels.

   You're looking for detail from the passage that supports the main idea—scientists make use of many different technologies to study the surfaces of other planets. Answer A) includes a specific detail about rovers, but does not offer any details that support the idea of multiple technologies being used. Similarly, answer D) provides another specific detail about space probes. Answer B) doesn't provide any supporting details; it simply introduces the topic of the passage. **Only answer C) provides a detail that directly supports the author's assertion that scientists use multiple technologies to study the planets.**

2. If true, which detail could be added to the passage above to support the author's argument that scientists use many different technologies to study the surface of planets?

   A) Because the Earth's atmosphere blocks x-rays, gamma rays, and infrared radiation, NASA needed to put telescopes in orbit above the atmosphere.

   B) In 2015, NASA released a map of Venus which was created by compiling images from orbiting telescopes and long-range space probes.

   C) NASA is currently using the Curiosity and Opportunity rovers to look for signs of ancient life on Mars.

   D) NASA has spent over $2.5 billion to build, launch, and repair the Hubble Space Telescope.

   You can eliminate answers C) and D) because they don't address the topic of studying the surface of planets. Answer A) can also be eliminated because it only addresses a single technology. **Only choice B) would add support to the author's claim about the importance of using multiple technologies.**

→

CONTINUE

3. The author likely included the detail *Earth-bound telescopes offer a distinct advantage over orbiting telescopes because they allow scientists to capture data from a fixed point* in order to:

**A)** Explain why it has taken scientists so long to map the surface of Venus.

**B)** Suggest that Earth-bound telescopes are the most important equipment used by NASA scientists.

**C)** Prove that orbiting telescopes will soon be replaced by Earth-bound telescopes.

**D)** Demonstrate why NASA scientists rely on many different types of scientific equipment.

**Only answer D) speaks directly to the author's main argument.** The author doesn't mention how long it has taken to map the surface of Venus (answer A), nor does he say that one technology is more important than the others (answer B). And while this detail does highlight the advantages of using Earth-bound telescopes, the author's argument is that many technologies are being used at the same time, so there's no reason to think that orbiting telescopes will be replaced (answer C).

# TEXT STRUCTURE

Authors can structure passages in a number of different ways. These distinct organizational patterns, referred to as **TEXT STRUCTURE**, use the logical relationships between ideas to improve the readability and coherence of a text. The most common ways passages are organized include:

- **PROBLEM-SOLUTION**: the author presents a problem and then discusses a solution.

- **COMPARISON-CONTRAST**: the author presents two situations and then discusses the similarities and differences.

- **CAUSE-EFFECT**: the author presents an action and then discusses the resulting effects.

- **DESCRIPTIVE**: an idea, object, person, or other item is described in detail.

## Example

The issue of public transportation has begun to haunt the fast-growing cities of the southern United States. Unlike their northern counterparts, cities like Atlanta, Dallas, and Houston have long promoted growth out and not up—these are cities full of sprawling suburbs and single-family homes, not densely concentrated skyscrapers and apartments. What to do then, when all those suburbanites need to get into the central business districts for work? For a long time it seemed highways were the answer: twenty-lane wide expanses of concrete that would allow commuters to move from home to work and back again. But these modern miracles have become time-sucking, pollution-spewing nightmares. They may not like it, but it's time for these cities to turn toward public transport like trains and buses if they want their cities to remain livable.

The organization of this passage can best be described as:

**A)** a comparison of two similar ideas

**B)** a description of a place

**C)** a discussion of several effects all related to the same cause

**D)** a discussion of a problem followed by the suggestion of a solution

You can exclude answer choice C) because the author provides no root cause or a list of effects. From there this question gets tricky, because the passage contains structures similar to those described above. For example, it compares two things (cities in the North and South) and describes a place (a sprawling city). However, if you look at the overall organization of the passage, you can see that it starts by presenting a problem (transportation) and then presents a solution (trains and buses), making **answer D) the only choice that encompasses the entire passage.**

# THE AUTHOR'S PURPOSE

Whenever an author writes a text, she always has a purpose, whether that's to entertain, inform, explain, or persuade. A short story, for example, is meant to entertain, while an online news article would be designed to inform the public about a current event.

Each of these different types of writing has a specific name. On the exam, you may be asked to identify which of these categories a passage fits into either by name or by general purpose:

- Narrative writing tells a story (novel, short story, play).
- Expository writing informs people (newspaper and magazine articles).
- Technical writing explains something (product manual, directions).
- Persuasive writing tries to convince the reader of something (opinion column on a blog).

You may also be asked about primary and secondary sources. These terms describe not the writing itself but the author's relationship to the topic. A primary source is an unaltered piece of writing that was composed during the time when the events being described took place; these texts are often written by the people involved. A secondary source might address the same topic but provides extra commentary or analysis. These texts can be written by people not directly involved in the events. For example, a book written by a political candidate to inform people about his or her stand on an issue is a primary source; an online article written by a journalist analyzing how that position will affect the election is a secondary source.

## Example

Elizabeth closed her eyes and braced herself on the armrests that divided her from her fellow passengers. Take-off was always the worst part for her. The revving of the engines, the way her stomach dropped as the plane lurched upward: it made her feel sick. Then, she had to watch the world fade away beneath her, getting smaller and smaller until it was just her and the clouds hurtling through the sky. Sometimes (but only sometimes) it just had to be endured, though. She focused on the thought of her sister's smiling face and her new baby nephew as the plane slowly pulled onto the runway.

The passage above is reflective of which type of writing?

**A)** narrative

**B)** expository

**C)** technical

**D)** persuasive

**The passage is telling a story—we meet Elizabeth and learn about her fear of flying—so it's a narrative text.** There is no factual information presented or explained, nor is the author trying to persuade the reader.

## FACTS VS. OPINIONS

On reading passages you might be asked to identify a statement in a passage as either a fact or an opinion, so you'll need to know the difference between the two. A FACT is a statement or thought that can be proven to be true. The statement *Wednesday comes after Tuesday* is a fact—you can point to a calendar to prove it. In contrast, an OPINION is an assumption that is not based in fact and cannot be proven to be true. The assertion that *television is more entertaining than feature films* is an opinion—people will disagree on this, and there's no reference you can use to prove or disprove it.

---

**✔**

Which of the following words would be associated with opinions?

- for example . . .
- studies have shown . . .
- I believe . . .
- in fact . . .
- the best/worst . . .
- it's possible that . .

---

## Example

Exercise is critical for healthy development in children. Today, there is an epidemic of unhealthy children in the United States who will face health problems in adulthood due to poor diet and lack of exercise as children. This is a problem for all Americans, especially with the rising cost of healthcare.

It is vital that school systems and parents encourage their children to engage in a minimum of thirty minutes of cardiovascular exercise each day, mildly increasing their heart rate for a sustained period. This is proven to decrease the likelihood of developmental diabetes, obesity, and a multitude of other health problems. Also, children need a proper diet rich in fruits and vegetables so that they can grow and develop physically, as well as learn healthy eating habits early on.

Which of the following is a fact in the passage, not an opinion?

A) Fruits and vegetables are the best way to help children be healthy.

B) Children today are lazier than they were in previous generations.

C) The risk of diabetes in children is reduced by physical activity.

D) Children should engage in thirty minutes of exercise a day.

Keep an eye out for answer choices that may be facts, but which are not stated or discussed in the passage.

Choice B) can be discarded immediately because it is negative and is not discussed anywhere in the passage. Answers A) and D) are both opinions—the author is promoting exercise, fruits, and vegetables as a way to make children healthy. (Notice that these incorrect answers contain words that hint at being an opinion such as *best, should*, or other comparisons.) **Answer B), on the other hand, is a simple fact stated by the author; it's introduced by the word *proven* to indicate that you don't need to just take the author's word for it.**

## DRAWING CONCLUSIONS

In addition to understanding the main idea and factual content of a passage, you'll also be asked to take your analysis one step further and anticipate what other information could logically be added to the passage. In a non-fiction passage, for example, you might be asked which statement the author of the passage would agree with. In an excerpt from a fictional work, you might be asked to anticipate what the character would do next.

To answer these questions, you need to have a solid understanding of the topic, theme, and main idea of the passage; armed with this information, you can figure out which of the answer choices best fits within those criteria (or alternatively, which ones do not). For example, if the author of the passage is advocating for safer working conditions in textile factories, any supporting details that would be added to the passage should support that idea. You might add sentences that contain information about the number of accidents that occur in textile factories or that outline a new plan for fire safety.

### Examples

Today, there is an epidemic of unhealthy children in the United States who will face health problems in adulthood due to poor diet and lack of exercise during their childhood. This is a problem for all Americans, as adults with chronic health issues are adding to the rising cost of healthcare. A child who grows up living an unhealthy lifestyle is likely to become an adult who does the same.

Because exercise is critical for healthy development in children, it is vital that school systems and parents encourage their children to engage in a minimum of thirty minutes of cardiovascular exercise each day. Even this small amount of exercise has been proven to decrease the likelihood that young people will develop diabetes, obesity, and other health issues as adults. In addition to exercise, children need a proper diet rich in fruits and vegetables so that they can grow and develop physically. Starting a good diet early also teaches children healthy eating habits they will carry into adulthood.

1. The author of this passage would most likely agree with which statement?

    A) Parents are solely responsible for the health of their children.

    B) Children who do not want to exercise should not be made to.

    C) Improved childhood nutrition will help lower the amount Americans spend on healthcare.

    D) It's not important to teach children healthy eating habits because they will learn them as adults.

**The author would most likely support answer C): he mentions in the first paragraph that unhealthy habits are adding to the rising cost of healthcare.** The main idea of the passage is that nutrition and exercise are important for children, so answer B) doesn't make sense—the author would likely support measures to encourage children to exercise. Answers A) and D) can also be eliminated because they are directly contradicted in the text. The author specifically mentions the role of schools systems, so he doesn't believe parents are solely responsible for their children's health. He also specifically states that children who grow up with unhealthy habit will become adults with unhealthy habits, which
contradicts D).

Elizabeth closed her eyes and braced herself on the armrests that divided her from her fellow passengers. Take-off was always the worst part for her. The revving of the engines, the way her stomach dropped as the plane lurched upward: it made her feel sick. Then, she had to watch the world fade away beneath her, getting smaller and smaller until it was just her and the clouds hurtling through the sky. Sometimes (but only sometimes) it just had to be endured,
though. She focused on the thought of her sister's smiling face and her new baby nephew as the plane slowly pulled onto the runway.

2. Which of the following is Elizabeth least likely to do in the future?

    A) Take a flight to her brother's wedding.

    B) Apply for a job as a flight attendant.

    C) Never board an airplane again.

    D) Get sick on an airplane.

It's clear from the passage that Elizabeth hates flying, but it willing to endure it for the sake of visiting her family. Thus, it seems likely that she would be willing to get on a plane for her brother's wedding, making A) and C) incorrect answers. The passage also explicitly tells us that she feels sick on planes, so D) is likely to happen. **We can infer, though, that she would not enjoy being on an airplane for work, so she's very unlikely to apply for a job as a flight attendant, which is choice B).**

## MEANING OF WORDS AND PHRASES

On the Reading section you may also be asked to provide definitions or intended meanings for words within passages. You may have never encountered some of these words before the test, but there are tricks you can use to figure out what they mean.

### Context Clues

The most fundamental vocabulary skill is using the context in which a word is used to determine its meaning. Your ability to observe sentences closely is extremely useful when it comes to understanding new vocabulary words.

There are two types of context that can help you understand the meaning of unfamiliar words: situational context and sentence context. Regardless of which context is present, these types of questions are not really testing your knowledge of vocabulary; rather, they test your ability to comprehend the meaning of a word through its usage.

SITUATIONAL CONTEXT is context that is presented by the setting or circumstances in which a word or phrase occurs. SENTENCE CONTEXT occurs within the specific sentence that contains the vocabulary word. To figure out words using sentence context clues, you should first determine the most important words in the sentence.

There are four types of clues that can help you understand context, and therefore the meaning of a word:

- RESTATEMENT clues occur when the definition of the word is clearly stated in the sentence.
- POSITIVE/NEGATIVE CLUES can tell you whether a word has a positive or negative meaning.
- CONTRAST CLUES include the opposite meaning of a word. Words like *but, on the other hand,* and *however* are tip-offs that a sentence contains a contrast clue.
- SPECIFIC DETAIL CLUES provide a precise detail that can help you understand the meaning of the word.

It is important to remember that more than one of these clues can be present in the same sentence. The more there are, the easier it will be to determine the meaning of the word. For example, the following sentence uses both restatement and positive/negative clues: *Janet suddenly found herself destitute, so poor she could barely afford to eat.* The second part of the sentence clearly indicates that *destitute* is a negative word. It also restates the meaning: very poor.

## Examples

*Select the answer that most closely matches the definition of the underlined word or phrase as it is used in the sentence.*

1. I had a hard time reading her <u>illegible</u> handwriting.

   A) neat

   B) unsafe

   C) sloppy

   D) educated

   Already, you know that this sentence is discussing something that is hard to read. Look at the word that illegible is describing: handwriting. Based on context clues, you can tell that illegible means that her handwriting is hard to read.

   Next, look at the answer choices. Choice A), *neat*, is obviously a wrong answer because neat handwriting would not be difficult to read. Choices B) and D), *unsafe* and *educated*, don't make sense. **Therefore, choice C), *sloppy*, is the best answer.**

2. The dog was <u>dauntless</u> in the face of danger, braving the fire to save the girl trapped inside the building.

   A) difficult

   B) fearless

   C) imaginative

   D) startled

   **Demonstrating bravery in the face of danger would be B) fearless.** In this case, the restatement clue (braving the fire) tells you exactly what the word means.

3. Beth did not spend any time preparing for the test, but Tyrone kept a <u>rigorous</u> study schedule.

   A) strict

   B) loose

   C) boring

   D) strange

   In this case, the contrast word *but* tells us that Tyrone studied in a different way than Beth, which means It's a contrast clue. If Beth did not study hard, then Tyrone did. **The best answer, therefore, is choice A).**

## Analyzing Words

As you no doubt know, determining the meaning of a word can be more complicated than just looking in a dictionary. A word might have more than one DENOTATION, or definition; which one the author intends can only be judged by looking at the surrounding text. For example, the word *quack* can refer to the sound a duck makes, or to a person who publicly pretends to have a qualification which he or she does not actually possess.

A word may also have different CONNOTATIONS, which are the implied meanings and emotion a word evokes in the reader. For example, a cubicle is a simply a walled desk in an office, but for many the word implies a constrictive, uninspiring workplace. Connotations can vary greatly between cultures and even between individuals.

Lastly, authors might make use of FIGURATIVE LANGUAGE, which is the use of a word to imply something other than the word's literal definition. This is often done by comparing two things. If you say *I felt like a butterfly when I got a new haircut*, the listener knows you don't resemble an insect but instead felt beautiful and transformed.

## Examples

*Select the answer that most closely matches the definition of the underlined word or phrase as it is used in the sentence.*

1. The uneven <u>pupils</u> suggested that brain damage was possible.

    **A)** part of the eye

    **B)** student in a classroom

    **C)** walking pace

    **D)** breathing sounds

**Only answer choice A (part of the eye) matches both the definition of the word and context of the sentence.** Choice B is an alternative definition for pupil, but does make sense in the sentence. Both C and D could be correct in the context of the sentence, but neither is a definition of pupil.

2. Aiden examined the antique lamp and worried that he had been <u>taken for a ride</u>. He had paid a lot for the vintage lamp, but it looked like it was worthless.

    **A)** transported

    **B)** forgotten

    **C)** deceived

    **D)** hindered

It's clear from the context of the sentence that Aiden was not literally taken for a ride. Instead, this phrase is an example of figurative language. **From context clues it can be figured out that Aiden paid too much for the lamp, so he was deceived (answer choice C).**

CONTINUE

Can you figure out the definition of the following words using their parts?

- ambidextrous
- anthropology
- egocentric
- diagram
- hemisphere
- homicide
- metamorphosis
- nonsense
- portable
- rewind
- submarine
- triangle
- unicycle

## Word Structure

Although you are not expected to know every word in the English language for your test, you will need the ability to use deductive reasoning to find the choice that is the best match for the word in question, which is why we are going to explain how to break a word into its parts to determine its meaning. Many words can be broken down into three main parts:

PREFIX — ROOT — SUFFIX

ROOTS are the building blocks of all words. Every word is either a root itself or has a root. Just as a plant cannot grow without roots, neither can vocabulary, because a word must have a root to give it meaning. The root is what is left when you strip away all the prefixes and suffixes from a word. For example, in the word *unclear*, if you take away the prefix *un-*, you have the root *clear*.

Roots are not always recognizable words, because they generally come from Latin or Greek words, such as *nat*, a Latin root meaning born. The word *native*, which means a person born in a referenced placed, comes from this root, so does the word *prenatal*, meaning before birth. It's important to keep in mind, however, that roots do not always match the exact definitions of words, and they can have several different spellings.

PREFIXES are syllables added to the beginning of a word and SUFFIXES are syllables added to the end of the word. Both carry assigned meanings and can be attached to a word to completely change the word's meaning or to enhance the word's original meaning.

Let's use the word prefix itself as an example: *fix* means to place something securely and *pre-* means before. Therefore, *prefix* means to place something before or in front. Now let's look at a suffix: in the word *feminism*, *femin* is a root which means female. The suffix *-ism* means act, practice, or process. Thus, *feminism* is the process of establishing equal rights for women.

Although you cannot determine the meaning of a word by a prefix or suffix alone, you can use this knowledge to eliminate answer choices; understanding whether the word is positive or negative can give you the partial meaning of the word.

Table 2.1. Common roots and affixes

| ROOT | DEFINITION | EXAMPLE |
| --- | --- | --- |
| ast(er) | star | asteroid, astronomy |
| audi | hear | audience, audible |
| auto | self | automatic, autograph |
| bene | good | beneficent, benign |
| bio | life | biology, biorhythm |
| chrono | time | chronometer, chronic |
| dict | say | dictionary, dictation |
| duc | lead or make | ductile, produce |
| gen | give birth | generation, genetics |
| geo | earth | geography, geometry |
| graph | write | graphical, autograph |
| jur or jus | law | justice, jurisdiction |
| log or logue | thought | logic, logarithm |
| luc | light | lucidity |
| man | hand | manual |
| mand | order | remand |
| mis | send | transmission |
| path | feel | pathology |
| phil | love | philanthropy |
| phon | sound | phonograph |
| port | carry | export |
| qui | quiet | quiet |
| scrib or script | write | scribe, transcript |
| sense or sent | feel | sentiment |
| tele | far away | telephone |
| terr | earth | terrace |
| vac | empty | vacant |
| vid | see | video |
| vis | see | vision |
| omni | all | omnivores |
| cap | take | capture |
| ced | yield | secede |
| corp | body | corporeal |
| demo | people | democracy |
| grad | step | graduate |
| crac or crat | rule | autocrat |
| mono | one | monotone |

| uni | single | Unicode |
|---|---|---|
| ject | throw | eject |

Table 2.2. Common prefixes

| PREFIX | DEFINITION | EXAMPLE |
|---|---|---|
| a- (also an-) | not, without; to, towards; of, completely | atheist, anaemic, aside, aback, anew, abashed |
| ante- | before, preceding | antecedent, ante-room |
| anti- | opposing, against | antibiotic, anticlimax |
| com- (also co-, col-, con-, cor-) | with, jointly, completely | combat, codriver, collude, confide |
| dis- (also di-) | negation, removal | disadvantage, disbar |
| en- (also em-) | put into or on; bring into the condition of; intensify | engulf, entomb |
| hypo- | under | hypoglycemic, hypothermia |
| in- (also il-, im-, ir-) | not, without; in, into, towards, inside | infertile, impossible, influence, include |
| intra- | inside, within | intravenous, intrapersonal |
| out- | surpassing, exceeding; external, away from | outperform, outdoor |
| over- | excessively, completely; upper, outer, over, above | overconfident, overcast |
| pre- | before | precondition, pre-adolescent, prelude |
| re- | again | reapply, remake |
| semi- | half, partly | semicircle, semi-conscious |
| syn- (also sym-) | in union, acting together | symmetry, symbiotic |
| trans- | across, beyond | transatlantic |
| trans- | into a different state | translate |
| under | beneath, below | underarm, undersecretary |
| under- | not enough | underdeveloped |

### Examples

*Select the answer that most closely matches the definition of the underlined word or phrase as it is used in the sentence.*

1. The <u>bellicose</u> dog will be sent to training school next week.

   **A)** misbehaved

   **B)** friendly

   **C)** scared

   **D)** aggressive

   Both misbehaved and aggressive look like possible answers given the context of the sentence. **However, the prefix *belli*, which means warlike, can be used to confirm that aggressive (choice D) is the right answer.**

2. The new menu <u>rejuvenated</u> the restaurant and made it one of the most popular spots in town.

   **A)** established

   **B)** invigorated

   **C)** improved

   **D)** motivated

   All of the answer choices could make sense in the context of the sentence, so it's necessary to use word structure to find the definition. The root *juven* means young and the prefix *re* means again, so rejuvenate means to be made young again. **The answer choice with the most similar meanings is *invigorated*, which means to give something energy.**

## COMPARING PASSAGES

In addition to analyzing single passages, the ACCUPLACER will also require you to compare two passages. Usually these passages will discuss the same topic, and it will be your task to identify the similarities and differences between the authors' main ideas, supporting details, and tones.

### Examples

*Read the following two passages and answer the following questions.*

#### Passage 1

Today, there is an epidemic of unhealthy children in the United States who will face health problems in adulthood due to poor diet and lack of exercise during their childhoods: in 2012, the Centers for Disease Control found that 18 percent of students aged 6-11 were obese. This is a problem for all Americans, as adults with chronic health issues are adding to the rising cost of healthcare. A child who grows up living an unhealthy lifestyle is likely to become an adult who does the same.

Because exercise is critical for healthy development in children, it is vital that school systems and parents encourage their children to engage in a minimum of thirty minutes of cardiovascular exercise each day. Even this small amount of exercise has been proven to decrease the likelihood that young people will develop diabetes, obesity, and other health issues as adults. In addition to exercise, children need a proper diet rich in fruits and vegetables so that they can grow and develop physically. Starting a good diet early also teaches children healthy eating habits they will carry into adulthood.

### Passage 2

When was the last time you took a good, hard look at a school lunch? For many adults, it's probably been years—decades even—since they last thought about students' midday meals. If they did stop to ponder, they might picture something reasonably wholesome if not very exciting: a peanut butter and jelly sandwich paired with an apple, or a traditional plate of meat, potatoes and veggies. At worst, they may think, kids are making due with some pizza and a carton of milk.

The truth, though, is that many students aren't even getting the meager nutrients offered up by a simple slice of pizza. Instead, schools are serving up heaping helpings of previously frozen, recently fried delicacies like french fries and chicken nuggets. These high-carb, low-protein options are usually paired with a limp, flavorless, straight-from-the-freezer vegetable that quickly gets tossed in the trash. And that carton of milk? It's probably a sugar-filled chocolate sludge, or it's been replaced with a student's favorite high-calorie soda.

*So what*, you might ask. Kids like to eat junk food—it's a habit they'll grow out of soon enough. Besides, parents can always pack lunches for students looking for something better. But is that really the lesson we want to be teaching our kids? Many of those children aren't going to grow out of bad habits; they're going to reach adulthood thinking that ketchup is a vegetable. And students in low-income families are particularly impacted by the sad state of school food. These parents rely on schools to provide a warm, nutritious meal because they don't have the time or money to prepare food at home. Do we really want to be punishing these children with soggy meat patties and salt-soaked potato chips?

1. Both authors are arguing for the important of improving childhood nutrition. How do the authors' strategies differ?

    A) Passage 1 presents several competing viewpoints while Passage 2 offers a single argument.

    B) Passage 1 uses scientific data while Passage 2 uses figurative language.

    C) Passage 1 is descriptive while Passage 2 uses a cause-effect structure.

    D) Passage 1 is friendly in tone while Passage 2 is angry.

The first author uses scientific facts (*the Centers for Disease Control found...* and *Even this small amount of exercise has been proven...*) to back up his argument, while the second uses figurative language (the ironic *delicacies* and the metaphor *sugar-filled chocolate sludge*), so **the correct answer is B).** Answer A) is incorrect because the first author does present any opposing viewpoints. Answer C) is incorrect because Passage 2 does not have a cause-effect structure. And while the author of the second passage could be described as angry, the first author is not particularly friendly, so you can eliminate answer D) as well.

2. Both authors argue that—

    **A)** children should learn healthy eating habits at a young age.

    **B)** low-income students are disproportionately affected by the low-quality food offered in schools.

    **C)** teaching children about good nutrition will lower their chances of developing diabetes as adults.

    **D)** schools should provide children an opportunity to exercise every day.

**Both authors argue children should learn healthy eating habits at a young age (answer A).** The author of Passage 1 states that *a child who grows up living an unhealthy lifestyle is likely to become an adult who does the same,* and the author of Passage 2 states that *many of those children aren't going to grow out of bad habits*—both of these sentences argue that it's necessary to teach children about nutrition early in life. Answers C) and D) are mentioned only by the author of Passage 1, and answer B) is only discussed in Passage 2.

# PART III: WRITING

The ACCUPLACER contains three writing tests: Sentence Skills, ESL – Language Use, and the WritePlacer, a short essay.

On the Sentence Skills test, you will be provided with a sentence and then asked to choose the best version of the underlined part of it. You will also be presented with a sentence and asked to rewrite it, with options provided in multiple-choice format. To answer correctly, use your skills in English grammar, punctuation, and sentence structure, which are reviewed below.

The ESL – Language Use test assesses your ability to use correct grammar in English-language sentences. You will need a strong grasp on parts of speech and sentence structure, including nouns, pronouns, pronoun agreement, verbs, subject-verb agreement, adjectives, adverbs, comparisons, and types of clauses.

For the WritePlacer, you will be presented with a prompt and asked to take a position on the issue discussed. Write a structured essay, comprised of multiple paragraphs, 300 to 600 words in length. Topics will likely be about issues affecting the daily lives of young people, like school policy or social matters.

The ACCUPLACER will consider five aspects of writing: focus, or how clearly you maintain your stance on the issue; organization, or your ability to clearly structure your essay and ideas; development and support, or your ability to develop your argument and present examples strengthening it; sentence structure, including correct and varied sentence construction; and mechanical conventions, including correct use of grammar and punctuation. A review of essential writing skills is in the following chapters.

# 5

# GRAMMAR

## PARTS OF SPEECH

### Nouns and Pronouns

NOUNS are people, places, or things. They are typically the subject of a sentence. For example, in the sentence *The hospital was very clean*, the noun is hospital; it is a place. PRONOUNS replace nouns and make sentences sound less repetitive. Take the sentence *Sam stayed home from school because Sam was not feeling well*. The word Sam appears twice in the same sentence. Instead, you can use a pronoun and say *Sam stayed at home because he did not feel well*. Sounds much better, right?

Because pronouns take the place of nouns, they need to agree both in number and gender with the noun they replaced. So, a plural noun needs a plural pronoun, and a feminine noun needs a feminine pronoun. In the previous sentence, for example, the plural pronoun *they* replaced the plural noun pronouns.

### Examples

Wrong: If a student forgets their homework, it is considered incomplete.

Correct: If a student forgets his or her homework, it is considered incomplete.

**Student is a singular noun, but their is a plural pronoun. So, this first sentence is grammatically incorrect. To correct it, replace their with the singular pronoun his or her.**

Wrong: Everybody will receive their paychecks promptly.

Correct: Everybody will receive his or her paycheck promptly.

**Everybody is a singular noun, but their is a plural pronoun. So, this sentence is grammatically incorrect. To correct it, replace their with the singular pronoun his or her.**

## SINGULAR PRONOUNS
- I, me, mine, my
- You, your, yours
- He, him, his
- She, her, hers
- It, its

## PLURAL PRONOUNS
- We, us, our, ours
- They, them, their, theirs

Wrong: When a nurse begins work at a hospital, you should wash your hands.

Correct: When a nurse begins work at a hospital, he or she should wash his or her hands.

**This sentence begins in third-person perspective and finishes in second-person perspective. So, this sentence is grammatically incorrect. To correct it, ensure the sentence finishes with third-person perspective.**

Wrong: After the teacher spoke to the student, she realized her mistake.

Correct: After Mr. White spoke to his student, she realized her mistake. (she and her referring to student)

Correct: After speaking to the student, the teacher realized her own mistake. (her referring to teacher)

**This sentence refers to a teacher and a student. But who does she refer to, the teacher or the student? To improve clarity, use specific names or state more specifically who spotted the mistake.**

## Verbs

Remember the old commercial, "Verb: It's what you do"? That sums up verbs in a nutshell. A verb is the action of a sentence; verbs "do" things. Verb must be conjugated to match the context of the sentence; this can sometimes be tricky because English has many irregular verbs. For example, runs is an action verb in the present tense that becomes ran in the past tense; the linking verb is (which describes a state of being) becomes was in the past tense.

Table 5.1. Conjugations of the verb *to be*

|  | PAST | PRESENT | FUTURE |
|---|---|---|---|
| **SINGULAR** | was | is | will be |
| **PLURAL** | were | are | will be |

As mentioned, verbs must use the correct tense, and that tense must make sense in the context of the sentence. For example, the sentence *I was baking cookies and eat some dough* sounds strange, right? That's because the two verbs *was baking* and *eat* are in different tenses. *Was baking* occurred in the past; *eat*, on the other hand, occurs in the present. Instead, it should be *ate some dough*.

Like pronouns, verbs must agree in number with the noun they refer back to. In the example above, the verb was refers back to the singular *I*. If the subject of the sentence was plural, it would need to be modified to read *They were baking cookies and ate some dough*. Note that the verb *ate* does not change form; this is common for verbs in the past tense.

Think of the subject and the verb as sharing a single s. If the noun ends with an s, the noun shouldn't and vice versa.

If the subject is separated from the verb, cross out the phrases between them to make conjugation easier.

### Examples

Wrong: The cat chase the ball while the dogs runs in the yard.

Correct: The cat chases the ball while the dogs run in the yard.

**Cat is singular, so it takes a singular verb (which confusingly ends with an s); dogs is plural, so it needs a plural verb.**

Wrong: The cars that had been recalled by the manufacturer was returned within a few months.

Correct: The cars that had been recalled by the manufacturer were returned within a few months.

**Sometimes, the subject and verb are separated by clauses or phrases. Here, the subject cars is separated from the verb phrase were returned, making it more difficult to conjugate the verb.**

Correct: The deer hid in the trees.

Correct: The deer are not all the same size.

**The subject of these sentences is a collective noun, which describes a group of people or items. This noun can be singular if its referring to the group as a whole or plural if it refers to each item in the group as a separate entity.**

Correct: The doctor and nurse work in the hospital.

Correct: Neither the nurse nor her boss was scheduled to take a vacation.

Correct: Either the patient or her parents need to sign the release forms.

**When the subject contains two or more nouns connected by and, that subject is plural and requires a plural verb. Singular subjects joined by or, either/or, neither/nor, or not only/ but also remain singular; when these words join plural and singular subjects, the verb should match the closest subject.**

Wrong: Because it will rain during the party last night, we had to move the tables inside.

Correct: Because it rained during the party last night, we had to move the tables inside.

**All the verb tenses in a sentence need to agree both with each other and with the other information in the sentence. In the first sentence above, the tense doesn't match the other information in the sentence: last night indicates the past (rained) not the future (will rain).**

## Adjectives and Adverbs

Adjectives are words that describe a noun. Take the sentence The boy hit the ball. If you want to know more about the noun *boy*, then you could use an adjective to describe it: *The little boy hit the ball.* An adjective simply provides more information about a noun or subject in a sentence.

For some reason, many people have a difficult time with adverbs, but don't worry! They are really quite simple. Adverbs and adjectives are similar because they provide more information about a part of a sentence; however, they do not describe nouns—that's an adjective's job. Instead, adverbs describe verbs, adjectives, and even other adverbs. For example, in the sentence *The doctor had recently hired a new employee*, the adverb *recently* tells us more about how the action *hired* took place.

Adjectives, adverbs, and modifying phrases (groups of words that together modify another word) should always be placed as close as possible to the word they modify. Separating words from their modifiers can create incorrect or confusing sentences.

### Examples

Wrong: Running through the hall, the bell rang and the student knew she was late.

Correct: Running through the hall, the student heard the bell ring and knew she was late.

**The phrase running through the hall should be placed next to student, the noun it modifies.**

Wrong: Of my two friends, Clara is the most smartest.

Correct: Of my two friends, Clara is more smart.

**The first sentence above has two mistakes. First, the word most should only be used when comparing three or more things. Second, the adjective should only be modified with more/most or the suffix -er/-est, not both.**

## Other Parts of Speech

Prepositions express the location of a noun or pronoun in relation to other words and phrases in a sentence. For example, in the sentence *The nurse parked her car in a parking garage*, the preposition *in* describes the position of the car in relation to the garage. The noun that follows the preposition is called it's object. In the example above, the object of the preposition *in* is the noun *parking garage*.

See *Phrases and Clauses* for more on independent and dependent clauses.

Conjunctions connect words, phrases, and clauses. The conjunctions summarized in the acronym FANBOYS—*for, and, nor, but, or, yet, so*—are called coordinating conjunctions and are used to join independent clauses. For example, in the sentence *The nurse prepared the patient for surgery, and the doctor performed the surgery*, the conjunction *and* joins together the two independent clauses. Subordinating conjunctions like *although*, *because*, and *if* join together an independent and dependent clause. In the sentence *She had to ride the subway because her car was broken*, the conjunction *because* joins together the two clauses.

Interjections, like *wow* and *hey*, express emotion and are most commonly used in conversation and casual writing.

## CONSTRUCTING SENTENCES

### Phrases and Clauses

A PHRASE is a group of words acting together that contain either a subject or verb, but not both. Phrases can be made from many different parts of speech. For example, a prepositional phrases includes a preposition and the object of that preposition (e.g., under the table), and a verb phrase includes the main verb and any helping verbs (e.g., had been running). Phrases cannot stand along as a sentence.

A CLAUSE is a group of words that contains both a subject and a verb. There are two types of clauses: independent clauses can stand alone as a sentence, and dependent clauses cannot stand alone. Dependent clauses begin with a subordinating conjunction.

### Examples

Classify each of the following as a phrase, independent clause, or dependent clause:

1. I have always wanted to drive a bright red sports car

2. under the bright sky filled with stars

3. because my sister is running late

**Number 1 is an independent clause—it has a subject (I) and a verb (have wanted) and has no subordinating conjunction. Number 2 is a phrase made up of a preposition (under), its object (sky), and words that modify sky (bright, filled with stars). Number 3 is a dependent clause—it has a subject (sister), a verb (is running), and a subordinating conjunction (because).**

### Types of Sentences

A sentence can be classified as simple, compound, complex, or compound-complex based on the type and number of clauses it has.

Table 5.2. Types of sentences

| SENTENCE TYPE | NUMBER OF INDEPENDENT CLAUSES | NUMBER OF DEPENDENT CLAUSES |
|---|---|---|
| Simple | 1 | 0 |
| Compound | 2+ | 0 |
| Complex | 1 | 1+ |
| Compound-complex | 2+ | 1+ |

A simple sentence consists of only one independent clause. Because there are no dependent clauses in a simple sentence, it can simply be a two-word sentence, with one word being the subject and the other word being the verb (e.g., I ran.). However, a simple sentence can also contain prepositions, adjectives, and adverbs. Even though these additions can extend the length of a simple sentence, it is still considered a simple sentence as long as it doesn't contain any dependent clauses.

Compound sentences have two or more independent clauses and no dependent clauses. Usually a comma and a coordinating conjunction (and, or, but, nor, for, so, and yet) join the independent clauses, though semicolons can be used as well. For example, the sentence My computer broke, so I took it to be repaired is compound.

Complex sentences have one independent clause and at least one dependent clause. In the complex sentence If you lie down with dogs, you'll wake up with fleas, the first clause is dependent (because of the subordinating conjunction if), and the second is independent.

Compound-complex sentences have two or more independent clauses and at least one subordinate clause. For example, the sentence Even though David was a vegetarian, he went with his friends to steakhouses, but he focused on the conversation instead of the food, is compound-complex.

## Examples

Classify: San Francisco in the springtime is one of my favorite places to visit.

**Although the sentence is lengthy, it is simple because it contains only one subject and verb (San Francisco... is) modified by additional phrases.**

Classify: I love listening to the radio in the car because I can sing along as loud as I want.

**The sentence has one independent clause (I love . . . car) and one dependent (because I . . . want), so it's complex.**

Classify: I wanted to get a dog, but I have a fish because my roommate is allergic to pet dander.

**This sentence has three clauses: two independent (I wanted . . . dog and I have a fish) and one dependent (because my . . . dander), so it's compound-complex.**

Classify: The game was cancelled, but we will still practice on Saturday.

**This sentence is made up of two independent clauses joined by a conjunction (but), so it's compound.**

**Clause Placement**

In addition to the classifications above, sentences can also be defined by the location of the main clause. In a periodic sentence, the main idea of the sentence is held until the end. In a cumulative sentence, the independent clause comes first, and any modifying words or clauses follow it. Note that this type of classification—periodic or cumulative—is not used in place of the simple, compound, complex, or compound-complex classifications. A sentence can be both cumulative and complex, for example.

**Examples**

Classify: To believe your own thought, to believe that what is true for you in your private heart is true for all men, that is genius.

**In this sentence the main independent clause—that is genius—is held until the very end, so it's periodic. It's also simple because it has one independent clause.**

Classify: We need the tonic of wildness—to wade sometimes in marshes where the bittern and meadow-hen lurk, and hear the booming of the snipe; to smell the whispering sedge where only some wilder and more solitary fowl builds her nest, and the mink crawls with its belly close to the ground.

**Here, the main clause—we need the tonic of wildness—is at the beginning, so the sentence is cumulative. It's also simple because it has one main clause.**

## PUNCTUATION

The basic rules for using the major punctuation marks are given in the following table.

Table 5.3. How to use punctuation

| PUNCTUATION | USED FOR | EXAMPLE |
| --- | --- | --- |
| Period | ending sentences | Periods go at the end of complete sentences |
| Question Mark | ending questions | What's the best way to end a sentence? |
| Exclamation Point | ending sentences that show extreme emotion | I'll never understand how to use commas! |
| Comma | joining two independent clauses (always with a coordinating conjunction) | Commas can be used to join clauses, but they must always be followed by a coordinating conjunction |
| | setting apart introductory and nonessential words and phrases | Commas, when used properly, set apart extra information in a sentence. |

| | separating items in a list | My favorite punctuation marks include the colon, semicolon, and period. |
|---|---|---|
| Semicolon | joining together two independent clauses (never with a conjunction) | I love exclamation points; they make sentences so exciting! |
| Colon | introducing a list, explanation or definition | When I see a colon, I know what to expect: more information. |
| Apostrophe | form contractions | It's amazing how many people can't use apostrophes correctly. |
| | show possession | Parentheses are my sister's favorite punctuation; she finds commas' rules confusing. |
| Quotation Marks | indicate a direct quote | I said to her, "Tell me more about parentheses." |

### Examples

Wrong: Her roommate asked her to pick up milk, and watermelon from the grocery store.

Correct: Her roommate asked her to pick up milk and watermelon from the grocery store.

**Commas are only needed when joining three items in a series; this sentence only has two (milk and watermelon).**

Wrong: The coach of the softball team—who had been in the job for only a year, quit unexpectedly on Friday.

Correct: The coach of the softball team—who had been in the job for only a year—quit unexpectedly on Friday.

Correct: The coach of the softball team, who had been in the job for only a year, quit unexpectedly on Friday.

**When setting apart nonessential words and phrases, you can use either dashes or commas, but not both.**

Wrong: I'd like to order a hamburger, from my favorite restaurant, but my friend says I should get a sandwich instead.

Correct: I'd like to order a hamburger from my favorite restaurant, but my friend says I should get a sandwich instead.

**Prepositional phrases are almost always essential to the sentences, meaning they don't need to be set apart with commas. Note that the second comma remains because it is separating two independent clauses.**

## CAPITALIZATION

- The first word of a sentence is always capitalized.
- The first letter of a proper nouns is always capitalized.

(We're going to Chicago on Wednesday.)

- The first letter of an adjectives derived from a proper noun is capitalized. (The play was described by critics as Shakespearian.)
- Titles are capitalized if they precede the name they modify. (President Obama met with Joe Biden, his vice president.)
- Months are capitalized, but not the names of the seasons. (Snow fell in March even though winter was over.)
- School subjects are not capitalized unless they are themselves proper nouns. (I will have chemistry and French tests tomorrow.)

### Example

Which sentence contains an error in capitalization?

A) She wrote many angry letters, but only senator Phillips responded to her request.

B) Matthew lives on Main Street and takes the bus to work every weekday.

C) Maria's goal has always wanted to be an astronaut, so she's studying astronomy in school.

D) Although his birthday is in February, Will decided to celebrate early by eating at Francisco's, his favorite restaurant.

**Sentence A) contains an error: the title senator should be capitalized when it's used in front of a name.**

## POINT OF VIEW

A sentence's **POINT OF VIEW** is the perspective from which it is written. Point of view is described as either first, second, or third person.

Table 5.4. Point of view

| PERSON | PRONOUNS USED | WHO'S ACTING? | EXAMPLE |
|--------|---------------|---------------|---------|
| first | I, we | The writer | I take my time when shopping for shoes. |
| second | you | The reader | You prefer to shop online. |
| third | he, she, it, they | The subject | She buys shoes from her cousin's store. |

Using first person is best for writing in which the writer's personal experiences, feelings, and opinions are an important element. Second person is best for writing in which the author directly addresses the reader. Third person is most common in formal and academic writing; it creates distance between the writer

Look for pronouns to help you identify which point of view a sentence is using.

and the reader. A sentence's point of view has to remain consistent throughout the sentence.

### Example

Wrong: If someone wants to be a professional athlete, you have to practice often.

Correct: If you want to be a professional athlete, you have to practice often.

Correct: If someone wants to be a professional athlete, he or she has to practice often.

**In the first sentence, the person shifts from third *(someone)* to second *(you)*. It needs to be rewritten to be consistent.**

## ACTIVE AND PASSIVE VOICE

Sentences can be written in active voice or passive voice. **ACTIVE VOICE** means that the subjects of the sentences are performing the action of the sentence. In a sentence in **PASSIVE VOICE**, the subjects are being acted on. So, the sentence *Justin wrecked my car* is in the active voice because the subject (*Justin*) is doing the action (*wrecked*). The sentence can be rewritten in passive voice by using a *to be* verb: *My car was wrecked by Justin*. Now the subject of the sentence (*car*) is being acted on. Notice that it's possible to write the sentence so that the person performing the action is not identified: *My car was wrecked*.

Generally, good writing will make more use of the active than passive voice. However, passive voice can sometimes be the better choice. For example, if it's not known who or what performed the action of the sentence, it's necessary to use passive voice.

### EXAMPLES

Rewrite the following sentence in active voice: *I was hit with a stick by my brother.*

**To rewrite a sentence in active voice, first take the person or object performing the action (usually given in a prepositional phrase) and make it the subject. Then, the subject of the original sentence becomes the object and the *to be* verb disappears: *My brother hit me with a stick.***

Rewrite the following sentence in passive voice: *My roommate made coffee this morning.*

**To rewrite a sentence in passive voice, the object (*coffee*) becomes the subject, and the subject gets moved to a prepositional phrase at the end of the sentence. Lastly, the *to be* verb is added: *The coffee was made this morning by my roommate.***

# TRANSITIONS

Transitions join together two ideas and also explain the logical relationship between those ideas. For example, the transition *because* tells you that two things have a cause and effect relationship, while the transitional phrase *on the other hand* introduces a contradictory idea. On the CBEST Writing section, you will definitely need to make good use of transitions in your essay.

Table 5.5. Common transition words

| CAUSE AND EFFECT | as a result, because, consequently, due to, if/then, so, therefore, thus |
|---|---|
| SIMILARITY | also, likewise, similarly |
| CONTRAST | but, however, in contrast, on the other hand, nevertheless, on the contrary, yet |
| CONCLUDING | briefly, finally, in conclusion, in summary, thus, to, conclude |
| ADDITION | additionally, also, as well, further, furthermore, in addition, moreover |
| EXAMPLES | in other words, for example, for instance, to illustrate |
| TIME | after, before, currently, later, recently, since, subsequently, then, while |

## Examples

Choose the transition that would best fit in the blank.

1. Clara's car breaks down frequently. _____, she decided to buy a new one.

2. Chad scored more points than any other player on his team. _____, he is often late to practice, so his coach won't let him play in the game Saturday.

3. Miguel will often his lunch outside. _____, on Wednesday he took his sandwich to the park across from his office.

4. Alex set the table _____ the lasagna finished baking in the oven.

A) however

B) for example

C) while

D) therefore

**Sentence 1 is describing a cause (her car breaks down) and an effect (she'll buy a new one), so the correct transition is therefore. Sentence 2 includes a contrast: it would make sense for Chad to play in the game, but he isn't, so the best transition is however. In Sentence 3, the clause after the transition is an example, so the best transition is for example. In Sentence 4, two things are occurring at the same time, so the best transition is while.**

# HOMOPHONES AND SPELLING

The ACCUPLACER will include questions that ask you to identify the correct **HOMOPHONE**, which is a set of words that are pronounced similarly but have different meanings. Bawl and ball, for example, are homophones. You will also be tested on spelling, so it's good to familiarize yourself with commonly misspelled words.

**COMMON HOMOPHONES**

- bare/bear
- brake/break
- die/dye
- effect/affect
- flour/flower
- heal/heel
- insure/ensure
- morning/mourning
- peace/piece
- poor/pour
- principal/principle
- sole/soul
- stair/stare
- suite/sweet
- their/there/they're
- wear/where

## Examples

*Choose the sentence that contains the correct spelling of the underlined word.*

1. Her excellent <u>manors</u> and friendly personality <u>made</u> it easy for her to win new clients.

2. Her excellent <u>manners</u> and friendly personality <u>made</u> it easy for her to win new clients.

3. Her excellent <u>manors</u> and friendly personality <u>maid</u> it easy for her to win new clients.

4. Her excellent <u>manners</u> and friendly personality <u>maid</u> it easy for her to win new clients.

People's behavior towards others are *manners*, while a *manor* is a country house. A *maid* is a person who cleans and *made* is the past tense of make. **So, the correct answer is 2.**

1. The nurse has three <u>patents</u> to see before lunch.

2. The nurse has three <u>patience</u> to see before lunch.

3. The nurse has three <u>patients</u> to see before lunch.

4. The nurse has three <u>pateince</u> to see before lunch.

**The correct spelling of *patients* is found in answer choice 3.**

# 6

# WRITING THE ESSAY

O n the ACCUPLACER, you will be asked to write one short essay, the WritePlacer. You will be presented with a prompt and asked to take a position on the issue discussed. Write a structured essay, comprised of multiple paragraphs, 300 to 600 words in length. Topics will likely be about issues affecting the daily lives of young people, like school policy or social matters.

The ACCUPLACER will consider five aspects of writing: focus, or how clearly you maintain your stance on the issue; organization, or your ability to clearly structure your essay and ideas; development and support, or your ability to develop your argument and present examples strengthening it; sentence structure, including correct and varied sentence construction; and mechanical conventions, including correct use of grammar and punctuation. A review of essential writing skills follows below.

## STRUCTURING THE ESSAY

There are many ways to organize an essay, and there are a few main things you can do to ensure that whatever structure you choose will work.

The first thing to realize is that there are many different kinds of essays. Each one has slightly different methods of delivering an idea, but they all have the same basic parts—introduction, body, and conclusion. The most common essay types are persuasive essays and expository essays. A persuasive essay takes a position on an issue and attempts to show the reader why it is correct. An expository essay explains different aspects of an issue without necessarily taking a side. Each of these essay types can be developed using various different methods.

## Introductions

Use an introduction and a conclusion that frame your argument or idea. The introduction is a good place to bring up complexities, counterarguments, and context, all things that will help the reader understand why you chose the idea you did. In the conclusion, revisit those issues and wrap all of them up.

Below is an example of an introduction for one of the thesis statements from the previous section. Note that it gives some context for the argument, acknowledges the opposite side, and gives the reader a good idea of what complexities the issue holds.

> Technology has changed massively in the last several years, but today's generation barely notices—high school students today are experienced with the internet, computers, apps, cameras, cell phones, and all kinds of technology. Teenagers need to be taught to use all these things safely and responsibly. Opponents of 1:1 technology programs might argue that students will be distracted or misuse the technology, but that is exactly why schools and teachers must teach them to use it. By providing technology to students, schools can help them use it for things such as creating great projects with other students, keeping in touch with teachers and classmates, and researching for class projects. In a world where technology is improving and changing at a phenomenal rate, schools have a responsibility to teach students how to navigate that technology safely and effectively, and providing each student with a laptop or tablet is one way to help them do that.

## The Body Paragraphs

Group similar ideas together and have a plan for paragraphs. You don't want to write one big chunk of a paragraph. Some ways to organize your essay include creating paragraphs that describe or explain each reason you give in your thesis; addressing the issue as a problem and offering a solution in a separate paragraph; telling a story that demonstrates your point (make sure to break it into paragraphs around related ideas); comparing and contrasting the merits of two opposing sides of the issue (make sure to draw a conclusion about which is better at the end).

Make sure that each paragraph is consistent inside— that there are no extra ideas that seem unrelated to the paragraph's main idea.

In the section entitled *Providing Supporting Evidence*, there is an example of a paragraph that is internally consistent and explains one of the main reasons given in one of the sample thesis statements above. Your essay should have one or more paragraphs like this to form the main body.

## Conclusions

In order to end your essay smoothly, write a conclusion that reminds the reader why you were talking about these topics in the first place. Go back to the ideas in the introduction and thesis sentence, but be careful not to simply restate your ideas.

Here is a sample conclusion paragraph that could go with the introduction written previously. Notice that this conclusion talks about the same topics as the introduction (changing technology and the responsibility of schools), but it does not simply rewrite the thesis.

> As technology continues to change, teens will continue to need to adapt to it. Schools already teach people how to interact and fit into society, so it makes sense that they would also teach how to fit technology into the equation of our lives. Providing students with their own devices is one step in that important task, and should be supported or encouraged in all schools.

# WRITING A THESIS STATEMENT

The thesis, a key organizational tool in any essay, tells readers specifically what you think and what you will say. Without a strong, direct thesis statement, your readers will have to deduce your main idea on their own.

Writing a good thesis sentence really comes down to one thing: simply state your idea and why you think it is true or correct.

### Example

*In your essay, take a position on this question. You may write about either one of the two points of view given, or you may present a different point of view on this question. Use specific reasons and examples to support your position.*

Many high schools have begun to adopt 1:1 technology programs, meaning that each school provides every student with a computing device such as a laptop or tablet. Educators who support these initiatives say that the technology allows for more dynamic collaboration and that students need to learn technology skills to compete in the job market. On the other hand, opponents cite increased distraction and the dangers of cyber-bullying or unsupervised internet use as reasons not to provide students with devices.

**Providing technology to every student is good for schools because it allows students to learn important skills such as typing, web design, or video editing, as well as giving**

students more opportunities to work together with their classmates and teachers.

I disagree with the idea that schools should provide technology to students because most students will simply be distracted by the free access to games and websites when they should be studying or doing homework.

In a world where technology is improving and changing at a phenomenal rate, schools have a responsibility to teach students how to navigate that technology safely and effectively, and providing each student with a laptop or tablet is one way to help them do that.

## PROVIDING SUPPORTING EVIDENCE

Your essay not only needs structured, organized paragraphs, it also needs to provide specific supporting evidence for your argument. Any time you make a general statement, it should be followed by specific evidence that will help to convince the reader that your argument has merit. The specific examples do not give new ideas to the paragraph; rather, they explain or defend the general ideas that have already been stated.

The following are some other examples of general statements and specific statements that provide more detailed support:

GENERAL: Students may get distracted online or access harmful websites.

SPECIFIC: Some students spend too much time using chat features or social media, or they get caught up in online games. Others spend time reading websites that have nothing to do with an assignment.

SPECIFIC: Teens often think they are hidden behind their computer screens. If teenagers give out personal information such as age or location on a website, it can lead to dangerous strangers seeking them out.

GENERAL: Many different types of animals can make good family pets.

SPECIFIC: Labrador Retrievers are friendly and enjoy spending time with the family, though it will be important to walk the dog often.

SPECIFIC: On the other hand, pets such as gerbils, mice, hamsters, or rats can be very affectionate and are much more contained—so it is easier to keep their living area clean.

## Example

*Below is an example of a paragraph that uses specific supporting ideas in a logical paragraph structure to support the thesis statement in the previous section.*

Providing students with their own laptop or tablet will allow them to explore new programs and software in class with teachers and classmates and then practice at home. In schools without laptops for students, classes have to visit computer labs, where they share old, used up computers that often have the keys missing or run so slowly they can barely be turned on before class ends. If a teacher tries to show students how to use a new tool or website, then students have to scramble to follow along and have no chance to explore the possibilities of the new tool. If they have laptops to take home instead, students can do things like practice editing video clips or photographs until they are perfect. They can email a classmate or use shared files to collaborate even after school. If schools expect students to learn these skills, it is their responsibility to provide students enough opportunities to practice them.

**This paragraph has some general statements:**

> *… their own laptop or tablet will allow them to explore new programs and software… and then practice…*

> *…it is their responsibility to provide… enough opportunities..*

**It also has some specific examples to back them up:**

> *…computers… run so slowly they can barely be turned on… students have to scramble to follow along and have no chance to explore…*

> *They can email a classmate or use shared files to collaborate…*

# WRITING WELL

The final considerations for your essay, the polish, if you will, add the touch that will help readers see your argument clearly and understand the complexity and depth of your writing.

## Transitions

Transitions are words, sentences, and ideas that help connect one piece of writing to another. You should use them between sentences and between paragraphs. Some common transitions include then, next, in other words, as well, in addition to. Be creative with your transitions, if possible, and make sure you understand what the transition you are using shows about the relationship between the ideas. For instance, the transition although implies that there is some contradiction between the first idea and the second.

## Syntax

The way you write sentences is important to maintaining the interest of a reader. Try to begin sentences differently. Make some sentences long and some sentences short. Write simple sentences.

Write complex sentences that have complex ideas in them. Readers appreciate variety.

There are four basic types of sentences: simple, compound, complex, and compound-complex. Try to use some of each type. Be careful that the sentences make sense, though—it is better to have clear and simple writing that a reader can understand than to have complex, confusing syntax that does not clearly express the idea.

## Word Choice and Tone

The words you choose influence the impression you make on readers. There are two important things you need to do. Firstly, use words that are specific, direct, and appropriate to the task—complex and impressive; simple and direct; or even neutral. Use the best words you know and do your best to avoid using vague, general words such as good, bad, very, or a lot. Words like these have unclear meanings from being used in many different situations —they can mean different things depending on the situation. Secondly, make sure that you actually use words you know! Trying to fit in too many "million-dollar words," may result in using some you do not know as well and thus use incorrectly; try to fit in words that you know make sense in the context.

## Editing, Revising, and Proofreading

When writing a timed essay, of course, you should not plan to have very much time for these steps; however, whatever time you have left after drafting should be spent looking over your essay and checking for spelling and grammar mistakes that may interfere with a reader's understanding. Some common mistakes to learn and look out for include subject/verb disagreement; confusing common words like *loose* and *lose*; pronoun/antecedent disagreement; comma splices and run-ons; or fragments.

# PART IV:
# TEST YOUR KNOWLEDGE

# 7

# PRACTICE TEST ONE

## ARITHMETIC

1. $5 - 3 \times 2 + 7 =$
   - A) 6
   - B) 11
   - C) 18
   - D) 22

2. $3.819 + 14.68 + 0.0006 =$
   - A) 5.2846
   - B) 18.4996
   - C) 18.505
   - D) 52.96

3. Which of the following is closest to $15,886 \times 210$?
   - A) 33,000
   - B) 330,000
   - C) 3,300,000
   - D) 33,000,000

4. A landscaping company charges 5 cents per square foot for fertilizer. How much would they charge to fertilize a 30 foot by 50 foot lawn?
   - A) $7.50
   - B) $15.00
   - C) $75.00
   - D) $150.00

5. $\frac{15}{25} =$
   - A) 0.06
   - B) 0.15
   - C) 0.375
   - D) 0.6

6. 15 is 8 percent of what number?
   - A) 1.2
   - B) 53.3
   - C) 120
   - D) 187.5

7. A woman's dinner bill comes to $48.30. If she adds a 20% tip, what will she pay in total?
   - A) $9.66
   - B) $38.64
   - C) $57.96
   - D) $68.30

8. In a neighborhood, $\frac{2}{5}$ of the houses are painted yellow. If there are 24 houses that are not painted yellow, how many yellow houses are in the neighborhood?
   - A) 16
   - B) 9.6
   - C) 24
   - D) 40

9. $54.48 \div 0.6 =$

   A) 0.908

   B) 9.08

   C) 90.8

   D) 908

10. $\frac{8}{15} \div \frac{1}{6} =$

    A) $\frac{4}{45}$

    B) $\frac{15}{48}$

    C) $\frac{16}{5}$

    D) $\frac{46}{15}$

11. Five numbers have an average of 16. If the first four numbers have a sum of 68, what is the fifth number?

    A) 12

    B) 16

    C) 52

    D) 80

12. The measures of two angles of a triangle are 25° and 110°. What is the measure of the third angle?

    A) 40°

    B) 45°

    C) 50°

    D) 55°

13. What percent of 14 is 35?

    A) 4.9

    B) 2.5

    C) 40

    D) 250

14. Megan has $\frac{13}{16}$ of a cake left. If her dad eats $\frac{1}{3}$ of the remaining cake, what proportion of the cake is left?

    A) $\frac{1}{4}$

    B) $\frac{13}{24}$

    C) $\frac{1}{2}$

    D) $\frac{3}{4}$

15. Which of the following is the greatest?

    A) 0.203

    B) 0.32

    C) 0.023

    D) 0.032

16. A restaurant employs servers, hosts, and managers in a ratio of 9:2:1. If there are 36 total employees, how many hosts work at the restaurant?

    A) 3

    B) 4

    C) 6

    D) 8

17. $1\frac{3}{4} + 2\frac{3}{8} =$

    A) $3\frac{3}{4}$

    B) $3\frac{7}{8}$

    C) 4

    D) $4\frac{1}{8}$

# ELEMENTARY ALGEBRA

1. What is the value of the expression $\frac{x^2 - 2y}{y}$ when $x = 20$ and $y = \frac{x}{2}$?

   A)  0

   B)  19

   C)  36

   D)  38

2. $3x^3 + 4x - (2x + 5y) + y =$

   A)  $11x - 4y$

   B)  $29x - 4y$

   C)  $3x^3 + 2x - 4y$

   D)  $3x^3 + 2x + y$

3. If $10y - 8 - 2y = 4y - 22 + 5y$, then $y =$?

   A)  $-30$

   B)  $-4\frac{2}{3}$

   C)  14

   D)  30

4. Which of the following lists of numbers is in order from least to greatest?

   A)  $\frac{1}{7}$, 0.125, $\frac{6}{9}$, 0.60

   B)  $\frac{1}{7}$, 0.125, 0.60, $\frac{6}{9}$

   C)  0.125, $\frac{1}{7}$, 0.60, $\frac{6}{9}$

   D)  $\frac{1}{7}$, 0.125, $\frac{6}{9}$, 0.60

5. Which of the following expressions is equivalent to $6x + 5 \geq -15 + 8x$?

   A)  $x \leq -5$

   B)  $x \leq 5$

   C)  $x \leq 10$

   D)  $x \leq 20$

6. Jane earns $15 per hour babysitting. If she starts out with $275 in her bank account, which of the following equations represents how many hours ($h$) she will have to babysit for her account to reach $400?

   A)  $400 = 275 + 15h$

   B)  $400 = 15h$

   C)  $400 = \frac{15}{h} + 275$

   D)  $400 = -275 - 15h$

7. At a bake sale, muffins are priced at $1.50 each and cookies are priced at $1 for two. If 11 muffins are sold, and the total money earned is $29.50, how many cookies were sold?

   A)  12

   B)  13

   C)  23

   D)  26

8. If $(2x + 6)(3x - 15) = 0$, then $x =$?

   A)  $\{-5, 3\}$

   B)  $\{-3, 5\}$

   C)  $\{-2, -3\}$

   D)  $\{-6, 15\}$

9. Adam is painting the outside of a 4-walled shed. The shed is 5 feet wide, 4 feet deep, and 7 feet high. How many square feet of paint will Adam need?

   A)  46

   B)  63

   C)  126

   D)  140

10. $4x + 3y = 10$

    $2x - y = 20$

    How many solutions $(x, y)$ are there to the system of equations above?

    A)  0

    B)  1

    C)  2

    D)  more than 2

11. $\frac{-6 + 11}{2(-3 - 8)} =$

    A)  $-\frac{5}{22}$

    B)  $-\frac{1}{2}$

    C)  $\frac{5}{22}$

    D)  $\frac{5}{9}$

**12.** $64 - 100x^2 =$

    **A)**   $(8 + 10x)(8 - 10x)$

    **B)**   $(8 + 10x)(8x + 10)$

    **C)**   $(8 - 10x)^2$

    **D)**   $(8 + 10x)^2$

# COLLEGE LEVEL MATHEMATICS

1. The graph of which of the following equations is a straight line parallel to the graph of
$3y - 1 = 2x$?

   A) $-3x + 2y = -2$

   B) $2x - 3y = 6$

   C) $-2x + 2y = 3$

   D) $-x + 3y = -2$

   E) $3x - 2y = 3$

2. If $16x^2 + 8x + 1 = 0$, then $x^3 = ?$

   A) $-\frac{1}{16}$

   B) $-\frac{1}{64}$

   C) $1$

   D) $16$

   E) $64$

3. If $f(x) = x^2 + 3$ and $g(x) = 3x - 12$, then $f(g(5)) = ?$

   A) $12$

   B) $28$

   C) $32$

   D) $72$

   E) $78$

4. What is an $x$-intercept of the graph $y = x^2 - 7x + 12$?

   A) $-4$

   B) $0$

   C) $3$

   D) $7$

   E) $12$

5. The sequence $\{a_n\}$ is defined by $a_1 = 5$ and $a_{n+1} = a_n + 7$ for $n = 1, 2, 3,\ldots$ What is the value of $a_5$?

   A) $12$

   B) $20$

   C) $26$

   D) $30$

   E) $33$

6. What is the value of the expression $0.5^x + 1$ when $x = -2$?

   A) $0.75$

   B) $1.25$

   C) $2$

   D) $4$

   E) $5$

7. Which of the following equations represents a line that passes through the points $(2, 7)$ and $(6, 10)$?

   A) $y = -\frac{3}{4}x + 5\frac{1}{2}$

   B) $y = -1\frac{1}{3}x - 4\frac{1}{2}$

   C) $y = \frac{3}{4}x + 5\frac{1}{2}$

   D) $y = \frac{4}{5}x - 5\frac{1}{2}$

   E) $y = 1\frac{1}{3}x + 2$

8. What is the value of the expression $|3x - y| + |2y - x|$ if $x = -4$ and $y = -1$?

   A) $-13$

   B) $-11$

   C) $11$

   D) $13$

   E) $24$

9. $\frac{n!}{(n-2)!} =$

   A) $n(n - 1)$

   B) $n$

   C) $\frac{n}{n-2}$

   D) $n^2$

   E) $\frac{n}{2}$

CONTINUE

**10.** $m = 5^{-a}$

$m = 4^{-b}$

$m = 3^{-c}$

$m = 2^{-d}$

The variables $a$, $b$, $c$, and $d$ each represent positive real numbers between 0 and 1. If $m$ is a constant, which of the following expressions is true?

A)   $a > b > c > d$

B)   $b > a > c > d$

C)   $c > d > b > a$

D)   $d > c > b > a$

E)   $a = b = c = d$

**11.** $\dfrac{(x^a y^b)(z^b y^a)}{z(xy)^a} =$

A)   $y^b z^{(b-1)}$

B)   $x y^b z^{(b-1)}$

C)   $x y^{ab} z$

D)   $\dfrac{y^b}{z^b}$

E)   $\dfrac{x^{2a}}{z^{(b-1)}}$

**12.** As shown below, 2 identical circles are drawn next to each other with their sides just touching; both circles are enclosed in a rectangle whose sides are tangent to the circles. If each circle's radius is 2 centimeters, find the area of the rectangle.

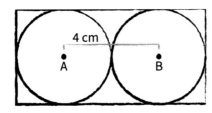

A)   8 cm²

B)   16 cm²

C)   24 cm²

D)   30 cm²

E)   32 cm²

**13.** If $y = \log_3 x$, what is the value of $y$ when $x = 81$?

A)   2

B)   4

C)   9

D)   27

E)   81

**14.** The county is instituting a new license plate system. The new plates will have 6 digits: the first digit will be 1, 2 or 3, and the next 5 digits can be any number from 0 – 9. How many possible unique combinations does this new system offer?

A)   53

B)   60

C)   $3 \times 10^5$

D)   $1 \times 10^6$

E)   $3 \times 10^6$

**15.** John and Jake are working at a car wash. It takes John 1 hour to wash 3 cars; Jake can wash 3 cars in 45 minutes. If they work together, how many cars can they wash in 1 hour?

A)   6

B)   7

C)   9

D)   12

E)   13

**16.** Let $f(x) = 2x + 1$. If $g(x)$ is obtained by reflecting $f(x)$ across the $y$-axis and translating it 4 units in the positive $y$ direction, what is $g(x)$?

A)   $g(x) = -2x + 3$

B)   $g(x) = -2x + 5$

C)   $g(x) = 2x + 5$

D)   $g(x) = 8x + 1$

E)   $g(x) = 8x + 5$

**17.** The points $(-1, -1)$, $(-3, -8)$, $(0, 6)$ and $(5, 11)$ are plotted on a coordinate plane. How many of these 4 points are collinear with the points $(0, 1)$ and $(2, 5)$?

A) 0

B) 1

C) 2

D) 3

E) 4

**18.** If $m\angle\beta < 90$ and $\cos\beta = \frac{\sqrt{3}}{2}$, then $\tan\beta=$?

A) $-\sqrt{3}$

B) $\frac{-1}{\sqrt{3}}$

C) $\frac{1}{\sqrt{3}}$

D) $1$

E) $\sqrt{3}$

**19.** $11, 7, 3, -1, \ldots$

If 11 is defined as the first term in the sequence given above, which of the following functions describes the sequence?

A) $f(n) = 11 + 4(n - 1)$

B) $f(n) = 11(4)^{(n-1)}$

C) $f(n) = 11 - 4n$

D) $f(n) = 15 - 4n$

E) $f(n) = 15 + 4(n + 1)$

**20.** A plane makes a trip of 246 miles. For some amount of time, the plane's speed is 115 miles per hour. For the remainder of the trip, the plane's speed is 250 miles per hour. If the total trip time is 72 minutes, how many minutes did the plane fly at 115 miles per hour?

A) 18

B) 23

C) 24

D) 28

E) 34

CONTINUE

# READING COMPREHENSION

*Directions for questions 1 – 12: Read the passage. Then choose the best answer to the question based on what you read.*

**1.** It could be said that the great battle between the North and South we call the Civil War was a battle for individual identity. The states of the South had their own culture, one based on farming, independence, and the rights of both man and state to determine their own paths. Similarly, the North had forged its own identity as a center of centralized commerce and manufacturing. This clash of lifestyles was bound to create tension, and this tension was bound to lead to war. But people who try to sell you this narrative are wrong. The Civil War was a not a battle of cultural identities— it was a battle over slavery. All other explanations for the war are a either a direct consequence of the South's desire for wealth at the expense of her fellow man or a fanciful invention to cover up this sad portion of our nation's history. And it cannot be denied that this time in our past was very sad indeed.

The main idea of the passage is that:

**A)** The Civil War was the result of cultural differences between the North and South.

**B)** The Civil War was the result of national division over slavery.

**C)** The North's use of commerce and manufacturing allowed it to win the war.

**D)** The South's belief in the rights of man and state cost them the war.

**2.** The most common way to measure body temperature is orally. A simple digital or disposable thermometer is placed under the tongue for a few minutes, and the task is complete. There are many situations, however, when measuring temperature orally isn't an option. For example, when a person cannot breathe through his nose, he won't be able to keep his mouth closed long enough to get an accurate reading. In these situations, it is often preferable to place the thermometer in the rectum or armpit. In fact, using the rectum provides a much more accurate reading than any other location does.

When a person cannot breathe well, it is best to take his or her temperature—

**A)** at a later time

**B)** orally

**C)** in the ear

**D)** rectally

**3.** Although it's a common disease, the flu is actually not highly infectious; that is, it is relatively difficult to contract. The virus can only be transmitted when individuals come into direct contact with the bodily fluids of people infected with it, often when they are exposed to expelled aerosol particles resulting from coughing and sneezing. Since these particles only travel short distances and the virus will die within a few hours on hard surfaces, it can be contained with simple health measures like hand washing and face masks.

The flu is not considered to be highly infectious because—

**A)** Many people who get the flu will recover and have no lasting complications, so only a small number of people who become infected will die.

**B)** The process of viral shedding takes two days, so infected individuals have enough time to implement simple health measures that stop the spread of the disease.

**C)** The flu virus cannot travel far or live for long periods of time outside the human body, so its spread can easily be contained if measures are taken.

**D)** Twenty-four hours is a relatively short period of time for the virus to spread among a population.

**4.** Mason was one of those guys who just always seemed at home. Stick him on a bus, and he'd make three new friends; when he joined a team, it was only a matter of time before he was elected captain. This particular skill rested almost entirely in his eyes. These brown orbs seemed lit from within, and when Mason focused that fire, it was impossible not to feel its warmth. People sought out Mason for the feeling of comfort he radiated, and anyone with a good joke would want to tell it to him. His laughter started with a spark in his eyes that ignited into his wide smile.

Which of the following is a logical conclusion that can be drawn from this description?

**A)** Mason wishes people would tell him more jokes.

**B)** Mason is very good at sports.

**C)** Mason does not like when strangers approach him.

**D)** Mason has many friends.

5. Skin coloration and markings play an important role for snakes: they help snakes attract mates and warn predators that the snake is poisonous. However, those markings may be misleading. Some snakes have a found a way to ward off predators without the actual venom. The California king snake, for example, has very similar markings to the venomous coral snake with whom it frequently shares a habitat. But the king snake is actually nonvenomous; it's merely pretending to be dangerous to eat. A predatory hawk or eagle, usually hunting from high in the sky, can't tell the difference between the two species, so the king snake gets passed over and lives another day.

What can the reader conclude from the passage above?

**A)** The king snake is dangerous to humans.

**B)** The coral snake and the king snake are both hunted by the same predators.

**C)** It is safe to handle snakes in the woods because it is easy to determine whether they are poisonous.

**D)** The king snake changes its markings when hawks or eagles are close by.

6. Recently jazz has been associated with New Orleans, but in the 1920s jazz was a booming trend whose influence affected many aspects of American culture. During this time period, major urban centers like New York and Chicago experienced new economic, cultural, and artistic vitality. Jazz music was played by and for a more expressive and freed populace than the United States had previously seen. Jazz music also provided the soundtrack for the explosion of African American art and culture now known as the Harlem Renaissance, during which numerous musicians promoted their distinctive music

as an integral part of the emerging African American popular culture.

The main idea of the passage is that

**A)** People should associate jazz music with the 1920s, not modern New Orleans.

**B)** Many famous jazz musicians began their careers in New York City and Chicago.

**C)** African Americans were instrumental in launching jazz into mainstream culture.

**D)** Jazz music played an important role in many cultural movements of the 1920s.

7. Providing adequate nutrition to patients is one of the most important responsibilities of healthcare facilities. Patients, like all people, have two basic nutritional needs: they require macronutrients, the carbohydrates, fats, and proteins that provide energy; and micronutrients, which are the vitamins and elements the body needs to function properly. A good diet will provide the appropriate amount of macronutrients, or calories, to keep patients energized and satiated without leading to weight gain, while also providing necessary amounts of micronutrients. Such a diet will help patients remain comfortable and heal properly. A poor diet, on the other hand, can make recovery significantly more difficult.

According to the passage, the nutritional needs of patients in acute and long-term care facilities—

**A)** are always determined by a medical formula that combines an appropriate ratio of macronutrients and micronutrients

**B)** vary depending on the patient

**C)** do not significantly affect the recovery of the patient; medication is more important

**D)** do not significantly vary from patient to patient

8. Credit scores are used by many institutions to evaluate the risk of providing loans, rentals, or services to individuals. Banks use credit scores when deciding when to approve loans; they can also use them to determine the terms of the loan itself. Similarly, car dealers, landlords, and credit card companies will likely all access your credit report before agreeing to do business with you. Even your

employer can access a modified version of your credit report (although it will not have your actual credit score on it).

The main idea of the passage is that:

**A)** Credit scores are used by many different institutions for many different types of interactions with individuals.

**B)** Your credit report is not private information.

**C)** Credit scores may be used by many different institutions in business and financial transactions with individuals.

**D)** It is important to have a good credit score in order to secure a loan.

9. The American love affair with popcorn began in 1912, when it was first sold in theaters. The popcorn industry flourished during the Great Depression by advertising popcorn as a wholesome food that the poor could afford. With the introduction of mobile popcorn machines, popcorn moved from the theater into fairs and parks and continued to rule the snack food kingdom until the rise in popularity of home televisions during the 1950s.

It wasn't until microwave popcorn became commercially available in 1981 that at-home popcorn consumption began to grow exponentially. With the wide availability of microwaves in the United States, popcorn also began popping up in offices and hotel rooms. The home still remains the most popular popcorn eating spot, where Americans eat seventy percent of the sixteen billion quarts of popcorn consumed annually in the United States.

It can be concluded from the passage above that:

**A)** People ate less popcorn in the 1950s than in previous decades because they went to the movies less.

**B)** Without mobile popcorn machines, people would not have been able to eat popcorn during the Great Depression.

**C)** People enjoyed popcorn during the Great Depression because it was a luxury food.

**D)** During the 1800s, people began abandoning theaters to go to fairs and festivals.

10. The bacteria, fungi, insects, plants, and animals that live together in a habitat have developed complex interspecies interactions known as symbiotic relationships. Ecologists characterize these interactions based on whether each party benefits. In mutualism both individuals benefit, while in synnecrosis both organisms are harmed. A relationship in which one individual benefits and the other is harmed is known as parasitism. Examples of these relationships can easily be found in any ecosystem. Pollination, for example, is mutualistic—pollinators get nutrients from the flower, and the plant is able to reproduce—while tapeworms, which steal nutrients from their host, are parasitic.

The author's primary purpose in writing this essay is—

**A)** to describe different types of symbiotic relationships.

**B)** to argue that interspecies relationships are harmful.

**C)** to explain how competition for resources results in long-term interspecies relationships.

**D)** to provide examples of the many different types of interspecies interactions

12. In 1860, the United States was in a state of turmoil over slavery; the presidential election that year between Lincoln and Douglas reflected that issue. Lincoln was vehemently against slavery; Douglas spoke in favor of states' rights, which included a state's right to determine the legality of slavery independently of the federal government. Major legislation had placed restrictions on slavery in the west and then lifted them. These developments played a key role in the presidential campaigns of the two candidates. Lincoln and Douglas met around the country in a series of debates reflective of the national mood. Ultimately Lincoln was elected to the presidency; Southern Secession and the Civil War would soon follow.

According to this passage, the differences between Lincoln and Douglas

A) led to the presidential election of 1860.

B) illustrated the tensions and division in the United States before the Civil War.

C) were a reason for the major legislation—later overturned—that had placed restrictions on slavery in the west.

D) led to the Civil War.

11. Following more than three centuries under Portuguese rule, Brazil gained its independence in 1822, maintaining a monarchical system of government until the abolition of slavery in 1888 and the subsequent proclamation of a republic by the military in 1889. Brazilian coffee exporters politically dominated the country until populist leader Getulio Vargas rose to power in 1930. By far the largest and most populous country in South America, Brazil underwent more than a half century of populist and military government until 1985, when the military regime peacefully ceded power to civilian rulers. Brazil continues to pursue industrial and agricultural growth and development of its interior. Exploiting vast natural resources and a large labor pool, it is today South America's largest economy and a regional leader. Pressing problems include high income inequality, crime, inflation, rising unemployment, and corruption.

*Courtesy CIA World Factbook 2015*

It can be inferred from the passage that

A) Brazil is controlled by the military.

B) Brazil is a poor country.

C) coffee has historically been an important agricultural resource in Brazil.

D) Brazil was the last South American country to abolish slavery.

*Directions for questions 13 – 22: Two sentences are shown and then followed by a question or a statement. Determine the best answer to the question or the best way to complete the statement.*

13. Many young adults are seeking jobs that offer benefits such as health insurance.

Some studies of people under twenty-eight show that these young adults value a high salary over health and retirement benefits.

What does the underlined sentence do?

A) It makes a contrast.

B) It expands on the first sentence.

C) It states an effect.

D) It reinforces the first.

14. Yoga is a proven means of stress relief.

In fact, it has been shown in scientific studies to reduce rates of heartburn, high blood pressure, and depression.

What does the underlined sentence do?

A) It makes a contrast.

B) It proposes a solution.

C) It gives an example.

D) It analyzes the statement made in the first.

15. A poor credit report can make it difficult to get a reasonable mortgage or car loan.

Fortunately, there are many options for credit repair, and it is possible to work with financial advisors to develop a plan to pay off loans and debts in order to improve your credit score.

What does the underlined sentence do?

A) It reinforces the first.

B) It proposes a solution.

C) It analyzes a statement made in the first.

D) It makes a contrast.

→ CONTINUE

16. Before the westward expansion of the United States, multitudes of buffalo—an important natural resource—roamed the Great Plains.

Enormous herds of buffalo migrated throughout the North American continent and supported the Native American tribes that dominated the terrain for centuries.

What does the underlined sentence do?

A) It states an effect.

B) It provides an example.

C) It proposes a solution.

D) It expands on the first sentence.

17. Young children require mental stimulation from an early age for their mental and behavioral growth.

Playing games and reading to small children helps with their cognitive development.

What does the underlined sentence do?

A) It draws a conclusion about what is stated in the first.

B) It makes a contrast.

C) It reinforces the first.

D) It proposes a solution.

18. An endangered species in the wild, pandas are supported and bred in zoos in their native China and elsewhere in the world.

Breeding programs have increased the panda population in captivity; Chinese, North American and European scientists collaborate in studying panda behavior to encourage breeding and population growth.

What does the underlined sentence do?

A) It states an effect.

B) It analyzes a statement in the first sentence.

C) It makes a contrast.

D) It expands on the first sentence.

19. Many teachers recommend that students study together in groups in order to practice quizzing each other on concepts and to discuss ideas and theories about which they may have questions.

Some students prefer to study alone because they find it difficult to focus on academic work in a group context, becoming distracted by discussions about social issues like sports and school events.

How do the two sentences relate?

A) They contradict each other.

B) They present a contrast.

C) They present a problem and a solution.

D) They present an argument and a supporting example.

20. More people are moving to Texas because of its strong economy, affordable housing, job opportunities, and limited state taxes.

In the fast-growing cities of Houston, Austin, and San Antonio, people are able to buy houses at more affordable rates than in cities like New York, Los Angeles or Chicago, making these Texas cities attractive destinations for young families.

How do the two sentences relate?

A) They establish a contrast.

B) They present a contradiction.

C) They reinforce each other.

D) They express roughly the same idea.

21. Many people work long hours and consequently eat too much processed or fast food, depriving them of adequate nutrition and providing them with too many empty calories instead.

Vitamin and mineral supplements are widely available at drugstores, and these products are usually very affordable; furthermore, there are multivitamins that contain essential minerals, so people need not take more than one capsule at a time.

How do the two sentences relate?

A) They present a problem and a solution.

B) They reinforce each other.

C) They express roughly the same idea.

D) They present a contradiction.

22. Many working Americans struggle with poverty despite having one or more jobs because their wages are not high enough to cover basic essentials like rent, food, and healthcare.

A higher minimum wage would allow more working Americans to improve their standard of living and ultimately save and invest money, strengthening the U.S. economy as a whole.

What does the second sentence do?

A) It proposes a solution.

B) It states an effect.

C) It makes a contrast.

D) It reinforces the first.

CONTINUE →

# SENTENCE SKILLS

*Directions for questions 1 – 12: In the following questions, select the answer that best rewrites the underlined portion of the sentence. Note that the first answer choice indicates no change was made to the sentence.*

1. Having finished her essay, washing the truck was the thing Maricela was ready to do.

    A) washing the truck was the thing Maricela was ready to do
    B) Maricela had another thing she was ready to do and that was washing the truck
    C) washing the truck Maricela was ready to do
    D) Maricela was ready to wash the truck

2. Many consider television to be eroding of our nation's imaginations.

    A) to be eroding of our nation's imaginations
    B) erosion of our nation's imaginations
    C) to erode our nation's imaginations
    D) to be eroding of the national imagination

3. Hearing a lot in the news that pet ownership is beneficial to health, especially for those with high blood pressure.

    A) Hearing a lot on the news that
    B) One often hears on the news that
    C) The news hears a lot that
    D) It is frequently heard in the news that

4. Raul, the most knowledgeable of us all, maintain that we would be needing better equipment.

    A) maintain that we would be needing
    B) maintains that we would be needing
    C) maintains that we would need
    D) maintain we would have needed

5. Does anyone have a guess that they would like to share before I reveal the answer?

    A) Does anyone have a guess that they would like
    B) Is anyone having a guess that they would like
    C) Do anyone have a guess that they would like
    D) Anyone with a guess would like

6. The meals at this restaurant have so much more salt in them than the restaurant we went to last week.

    A) The meals at this restaurant have so much more salt in them than the restaurant we went to last week.
    B) The meals at this restaurant are so much saltier than the restaurant we went to last week.
    C) The meals at this restaurant have so much more salt in them than that other restaurant.
    D) The meals at this restaurant have so much more salt in them than those at the restaurant we went to last week.

7. Even though she knew it would reflect badly, the politician withdrawing her statement.

    A) the politician withdrawing her statement
    B) the politician withdraws her statement
    C) the politician was going to withdraw her statement
    D) the politician withdrew her statement

8. The holiday Cinco de Mayo, a Mexican-American tradition which celebrates the Mexican repulsion of the French occupation.

    A) tradition which celebrates the Mexican repulsion of the French occupation
    B) tradition, celebrates the Mexican repulsion of the French occupation
    C) celebration of the Mexican repulsion of the French occupation
    D) celebrating of the Mexican repulsion of the French occupation

9. If you have <u>questions about the schedule, please be seeing your counselor.</u>

 A) questions about the schedule, please be seeing your counselor

 B) to ask the counselor your questions about the schedule

 C) questions about the schedule, please see your counselor

 D) a question about the schedule, be seeing your counselor

10. Tina and Marie <u>had never seen anyone eating so loud</u>.

 A) had never seen anyone eating so loud

 B) had never seen anyone eating so loudly

 C) never saw anyone eating so loud

 D) had never seen someone eating so loud

11. <u>It is so easy to be self-published these days; it seems as though everyone has a blog.</u>

 A) It is so easy to be self-published these days; it seems as though everyone has a blog.

 B) It is to easy to be self-published these days because it seems as though everyone has a blog.

 C) It is so easy to publish yourself these days; it seems as though everyone has a blog.

 D) It is so easy to be self-published these days; it seems as though everyone had a blog.

12. We reached the mountaintop and <u>was looking out at the view when the thunderstorm began</u>.

 A) was looking out at the view when the thunderstorm began

 B) were looking out at the incredible view when the thunderstorm began

 C) were in the middle of looking out at the view when the thunderstorm began

 D) were having looked out at the view when the thunderstorm began

*Directions for questions 13 – 25: Select the answer that begins to rewrite the following sentences most effectively and without changing the meaning of the original sentence. Keep in mind that not every answer choice will complete the original sentence.*

13. While shark attacks on humans are very rare, sometimes surfers look like seals on their boards, which can entice a passing shark.

 Rewrite, beginning with

 *Shark attacks on humans are very rare,—*

 The next words will be:

 A) but sometimes surfers

 B) and sometimes surfers

 C) even though sometimes surfers

 D) nevertheless sometimes surfers

14. The teacher saw no horseplay as he monitored the halls.

 Rewrite, beginning with:

 *As he monitored the halls,—*

 The next words will be:

 A) no horseplay could be seen.

 B) then the teacher saw no horseplay.

 C) and seeing no horseplay

 D) the teacher saw no horseplay.

15. It can be difficult to learn to play guitar, but the same cannot be said of the kazoo.

 Rewrite, beginning with:

 *Unlike the kazoo,—*

 The next words will be:

 A) it can be difficult to learn the guitar.

 B) we cannot easily learn the guitar.

 C) the guitar can be difficult to learn.

 D) the guitar is difficult to be learned.

CONTINUE

16. The whistle was sounded, and the kickoff began.

Rewrite, beginning with:

*The kickoff began—*

The next words will be:

A) after the whistle was sounded.

B) and the whistle was sounded.

C) although the whistle was sounded.

D) the whistle was sounded.

17. Although the world of *Harry Potter* is filled with magic and wonder, issues such as classism exist even in that fictional world.

Rewrite, beginning with:

*The world of Harry Potter is filled with magic and wonder,—*

The next words will be:

A) but issues such as classism exist

B) nevertheless issues such as classism exist

C) and issues such as classism exist

D) even if issues such as classism exist

18. It is unusual to see wild orcas alone, since they are social animals.

Rewrite, beginning with:

*Orcas are social animals,—*

The next words will be:

A) so it is unusual to see them alone in the wild.

B) wild orcas are not usually seen alone.

C) and seeing wild orcas alone is unusual.

D) so it is alone that wild orcas are not seen.

19. The show began, and everyone shuffled to their seats.

Rewrite, beginning with:

*Everyone shuffled to their seats—*

The next words will be:

A) beginning the show.

B) when the show began.

C) although the show began.

D) and the show began.

20. If he needs help with his schoolwork, he will get a tutor.

Rewrite, beginning with:

*He won't get a tutor—*

The next words will be:

A) if he needs help.

B) when he needs help.

C) although he needs help.

D) unless he needs help.

21. If I had the resources, I would buy an energy-efficient car.

Rewrite, beginning with:

*I cannot buy an energy-efficient car—*

The next words will be:

A) when lacking the resources.

B) because I lack the resources.

C) although there are the resources.

D) without lacking the resources.

22. After twenty minutes of "debate," Talia felt weary of Jacob's stubbornness.

Rewrite, beginning with:

*Talia felt weary of Jacob's stubbornness—*

The next words will be:

A) "debating" him for twenty minutes.

B) having "debated" him for twenty minutes.

C) and they "debated" for twenty minutes.

D) despite having "debated" him for twenty minutes.

23. Tortoises have life expectancies of over 180 years, much longer than humans' life expectancies.

Rewrite, beginning with:

*Unlike tortoises,—*

The next words will be:

A) humans can live

B) humans do not live

C) it is not easy to live

D) long lives are difficult

24. Kelli felt excited and nervous when she moved into her first apartment.

Rewrite, beginning with:

*Moving into her first apartment,—*

The next words will be:

A) excitement and nervousness were felt by Kelli.

B) when Kelli felt excited and nervous.

C) Kelli felt excited and nervous.

D) Kelli feeling excited and nervous.

25. The music began to play, and everyone started to dance.

Rewrite, beginning with:

*Everyone started to dance—*

The next words will be:

A) and the music

B) before the music

C) after the music

D) although the music

CONTINUE

# WritePlacer

*Write a multiple-paragraph essay of approximately 300 – 600 words based on the prompt below. Plan, write, review and edit your essay during the time provided, and read the prompt carefully before starting your essay.*

Vaccines have been one of the most powerful and effective advances in modern medicine. Throughout most of our history, humans could do little to prevent the spread of disease. Now, we have the ability to create in most people an immunity to specific viruses and bacteria. Concerns about vaccines remain, however. Many people claim a religious objection to medical interference, while others worry about the safety of the young children being vaccinated. Scientists argue in return that allowing a few to opt out of vaccination endangers the whole community by making it possible for these diseases to return. Since personal freedom is such an important part of our culture, we must decide how to balance the safety of the community with the ability of citizens to make decisions about their own bodies and those of their children.

Write an essay of 300 – 600 words taking a position on whether vaccines should be mandatory. Support your position using logic and examples.

# ESL – LANGUAGE USE

*Fill in the blank in the sentence with the word or phrase that forms a grammatically correct sentence.*

1.  She told them to _____ their room before they left for the party.

    A) cleaned

    B) tidy

    C) clears

    D) neat

2.  They left for the party, but Rebecca had to return home because _____ forgot her purse.

    A) he

    B) they

    C) we

    D) she

3.  I had worked a very long shift, _____ I still had to run errands after work.

    Which conjunction best completes the sentence?

    A) and

    B) or

    C) but

    D) so

4.  She hurried up that morning, _____ she wouldn't be late for her first day at work.

    Which word best completes the sentence?

    A) because

    B) for

    C) but

    D) so

5.  _____ the Eiffel Tower when he visited Paris.

    Which of the following best completes the sentence?

    A) They saw

    B) He seen

    C) They seen

    D) He saw

*Read the sentences and determine the best way to combine them.*

6.  With two bags to carry, Jim had a problem. His brother didn't have any.

    A) While his brother didn't have any, Jim had a problem with two bags to carry.

    B) With two bags to carry, Jim had a problem; his brother didn't have any.

    C) With two bags to carry, his brother didn't have any; Jim had a problem.

    D) Jim had a problem with two bags to carry because his brother didn't have any.

7.  The mother was worried. Her daughter was out late.

    A) Even though her daughter was out late, the mother was worried.

    B) While the mother was worried, her daughter was out late.

    C) The mother was worried because her daughter was out late.

    D) Before the daughter was out late, her mother had been worried.

8.  Brandon sighed as his car broke down. Jada tried to call a tow truck.

    A) Sighing as his car broke down, Jada tried to call a tow truck.

    B) Brandon sighed as his car broke down, so Jada tried to call a tow truck.

    C) Jada tried to call a tow truck, and Brandon sighed as his car broke down.

    D) While Brandon sighed as his car broke down and Jada tried to call a tow truck.

9.  Kim and Hai took the dog for a walk. The dog chased a butterfly.

    A) When Kim and Hai took the dog for a walk, the dog chased a butterfly.

    B) The dog chased a butterfly as Kim and Hai had taken it for a walk.

    C) Kim and Hai took the dog for a walk because it had chased a butterfly.

    D) The dog chased a butterfly because Kim and Hai had taken it for a walk.

10. Laura liked to come home and relax. Her brother, however, expected her to cook dinner.

   A) Her brother expected her to cook, and Laura wanted to relax.

   B) Even though he expected her to cook dinner, Laura liked to relax.

   C) Coming home to relax, Laura's brother expected her to cook.

   D) Laura liked to come home and relax, but her brother expected her to cook dinner.

11. The parents were upset. The house was a mess, and the kids were still awake.

   A) The parents were upset and the house was a mess and the kids were still awake.

   B) The parents were upset because the house was a mess and the kids were still awake.

   C) The house was a mess and the kids were still awake because the parents were upset.

   D) When the parents were upset, the house was a mess and so the kids were still awake.

12. One key to a healthy diet is eating fruits and vegetables. Avoid drinking sugary sodas.

   A) Key to a healthy diet is eating fruits and vegetables and to avoid sugary sodas.

   B) Eating fruits and vegetables is key to a healthy diet, so sugary sodas should not be drunk.

   C) It is key to eat fruits and vegetables for a healthy diet, and to avoid sugary sodas.

   D) Avoiding sugary sodas and eating vegetables and fruits are the keys to a healthy diet.

13. The children went to the park. They played baseball with their friends.

   A) The children went to the park to play baseball with their friends.

   B) The children went to the park when they were playing baseball with their friends.

   C) To go to the park, the children played baseball with their friends.

   D) The children went to the park while they played baseball with their friends.

14. Many homeowners use natural cleaning products. They argue that natural ingredients are just as effective as industrial soaps.

   A) Arguing that natural ingredients are just as effective as industrial soaps, more homeowners are switching to natural products made up of these ingredients.

   B) Many homeowners prefer to use natural cleaning products, which they argue are just as effective as industrial soaps.

   C) Many natural products can be used for cleaning, but homeowners are using them instead of industrial soaps.

   D) Homeowners can use natural alternatives to industrial soaps, which they may no longer want to use.

15. Many people feel that the air conditioning in offices is too strong. However, it is difficult to get building managers to change the temperature.

   A) While it is difficult to get building managers to change the temperature, many people feel that office air conditioning is too strong.

   B) Even though many people feel that office air conditioning is too strong, it is difficult to get building managers to change the temperature.

   C) It is difficult to get building managers to change the temperature because many people feel that the air conditioning in offices is too strong.

   D) When people feel that office air conditioning is too strong, it is difficult to get building managers to change the temperature.

16. Wanda's car broke down. She had to call a tow truck.

   A) Wanda's car broke down because she had to call a tow truck.

   B) To call a tow truck, Wanda's car broke down.

   C) When Wanda's car broke down, she had to call a tow truck.

   D) Breaking down, Wanda's car had to call a tow truck.

17. Two raccoons live in that tree. They ate the vegetables in my garden.

    A) The two raccoons live in that tree when they ate the vegetables in my garden.

    B) Eating the vegetables in my garden, two raccoons live in that tree.

    C) Because they live in that tree, two raccoons ate the vegetables in my garden.

    D) The two raccoons that live in that tree ate the vegetables in my garden.

18. Gabriel needs to study. Luciana turns off the TV.

    A) Gabriel needs to study after Luciana turns off the TV.

    B) Luciana turns off the TV, so Gabriel needs to study.

    C) Because Gabriel needs to study, Luciana turns off the TV.

    D) Before Gabriel needs to study, Luciana turns off the TV.

→

CONTINUE

# ESL – Reading Skills

1. Many phone companies offer families annual group rates to save money on telephone, internet and text message charges. However, customers often complain about extra fees that cause their phone bills to be higher than they had expected. Citizens have complained to their government representatives about unfair marketing and trade practices by communications companies in this regard. As a result, some phone companies have begun to simplify their billing practices. In addition, smaller phone companies have emerged that offer prepaid or monthly plans with fewer fees and more straightforward charges.

   From this passage, which of these statements can the reader assume?

   A) Phone companies are breaking the law.

   B) Government involvement has forced phone companies to make changes.

   C) Customers should not have complained to the government.

   D) Small phone companies cannot afford to compete with big ones.

2. In the U.S., the states of the Great Plains include North and South Dakota, Nebraska, Kansas, and Oklahoma. Parts of eastern Montana, Wyoming, Colorado, and New Mexico also fall within the Great Plains, as does northwestern Texas. Historically the Great Plains were home to millions of buffalo, which were hunted by Native Americans. As the United States grew, the land was conquered and buffalo were killed, making way for white settlers who used the land for cattle ranching and eventually agriculture. Railroads allowed farmers to sell their crops in cities more easily. Today, many people have left the states of the Great Plains to pursue careers and livelihoods where opportunities in business and technology are more abundant in major cities elsewhere in the United States. However, new opportunities have appeared in Plains cities like Omaha and Oklahoma City and in the oil and gas industry in North Dakota.

The Great Plains were originally—

A) home to Native Americans and vast herds of buffalo

B) settled by farmers and ranchers

C) divided into five states

D) a source of opportunities in business and technology

3. Roy and Leticia each work two jobs. Roy works for the water company as a technician and drives a taxi at night. Leticia is a medical assistant and takes care of her neighbor's children four nights a week, in addition to watching her own two sons. Once a week, Leticia goes to a medical class at the community college to improve her career opportunities. Both Roy and Leticia go to church on Sundays and participate in church activities on Sunday afternoons with their families.

   According to the passage, Leticia and Roy spend most of their time—

   A) working

   B) at church

   C) in medical class

   D) driving a taxi

4. Juan and his brother David own a business. Juan manages the money and works with clients, and David hires and manages the workers. Thanks to low taxes and high demand, their business is growing. Juan and David have both been able to buy houses for themselves and invest in better equipment for their business.

   From the passage, which of these statements can the reader assume?

   A) Juan and David do not work well together.

   B) David is not good at managing money.

   C) Juan is good at managing money.

   D) Juan is not good at managing people.

5. New York City can be a great place to raise a family. There are lots of parks and playgrounds for children, and plenty of good schools. It is easy for families of any income to get around on foot or using public

transportation. Moreover, New York has an abundance of cultural opportunities. With countless museums, galleries, theaters and musical performances year-round, it is one of the most diverse cities in the world.

*An abundance of opportunities* means—

A) limited opportunities

B) some opportunities

C) a lot of opportunities

D) a few opportunities

6. Jennifer is about to buy her first car. Since she drives every day, she wants a car that does not require a lot of gas or maintenance. Before going to look at cars, she spends several days researching different brands to find out which models are most reliable and efficient. She finally decides on three different types of cars that meet her needs and that she can afford. She plans to try driving each car to find out which one she is most comfortable driving.

Jennifer wants a car that does not need a lot of gas or maintenance because—

A) she drives every day

B) she does not have time to stop for gas every day

C) she is not comfortable with other models

D) she likes to do a lot of research

7. The Museum of Natural Science has opened an exhibit about the ecology of the Columbia River Basin. The exhibit includes plants, insects, birds, and mammals that are unique to the Columbia River Basin and explores the changes that have occurred in this delicate ecosystem over the last century. The exhibit has exciting audio-visual presentations. Individual tickets are available on the museum's website, and groups may apply for special ticket prices by calling the museum directly.

Which of the following is implied by the passage above?

A) The exhibit is about river ecosystems throughout North America.

B) The exhibit is very expensive for individuals.

C) The exhibit will not be open for very long.

D) The exhibit is interesting for visitors.

8. Today, school lunches consist of fried foods like french fries and chicken nuggets accompanied by defrosted vegetables that students often throw away. Many students drink sugary sodas or chocolate milk instead of water or calcium-rich, low-fat milk. Teachers and parents worry that children will grow up thinking that it is normal to eat these unhealthy meals every day. Furthermore, students in low-income families are particularly impacted by low-quality school food. Parents rely on schools to provide a warm, nutritious meal because they don't have the time or money to prepare food at home.

What is the main idea of this passage?

A) Many school lunches contain fried food.

B) Unhealthy school lunches pose a risk to students' long-term wellness, especially those students from low-income families.

C) Some families cannot afford to provide three warm meals a day and so rely on school lunches to help feed their children.

D) Unhealthy school lunches are a problem in many schools, especially those schools in low-income neighborhoods.

9. Football, or soccer as it is known in the United States, is probably the most popular sport in the world. Every four years, the World Cup brings together national football teams, even from countries that may historically be enemies or have bad political relationships. People put aside their differences to enjoy the exciting games and cheer on their national team. As teams are eliminated in games leading up to the final match, people around the globe take sides and support their favorite team as it plays for the ultimate prize: the FIFA World Cup Trophy.

The World Cup is played—

A) in the United States

B) only between countries that may be political rivals

C) every two years

D) every four years

10. Owning a cat is not difficult, but a few tips can help make life better for both you and your cat. First, it is a good idea to feed cats wet food twice a day; certain brands of wet cat food are especially high in protein, which is better for your cat's health than high-carbohydrate dry food. Second, be sure to clean your cat's litter box at least once a day. Otherwise, your cat may seek out another toilet in your home! In addition, be sure to take your pet for regular check-ups at the vet.

From this passage, which of these statements can the reader assume?

A) Cats prefer a clean living space.

B) Cats should not eat high-protein food.

C) Owning a cat is complicated and requires a lot of work.

D) Most people should not own cats.

11. Toussaint L'Ouverture was the leader of the Haitian Revolution, when slaves in Haiti rebelled against France, eventually winning their freedom and the independence of Haiti. L'Ouverture was a talented political and military leader, and he formed international alliances to support Haitian independence and freedom for the slaves. Although he died before independence was formally declared, his legacy continues as a fighter for justice and freedom.

What is the main idea of this passage?

A) Toussaint L'Ouverture was an important man.

B) Toussaint L'Ouverture was an important leader who fought for freedom in Haiti.

C) Toussaint L'Ouverture died before Haiti was formally independent.

D) Toussaint L'Ouverture was an important Haitian leader who formed alliances.

12. Some people enjoy giving presentations in front of a group, while others prefer to submit their work in a written document. These different approaches usually depend on an individual's personality. For example, a more outgoing person may enjoy capturing the attention of the crowd in a class or a meeting. In this case, he or she may wish to deliver a presentation about a recent project or assignment. On the other hand, someone who is shy or anxious about public speaking may feel uncomfortable standing up in front of a group of people. These individuals would rather spend more time writing up a report to submit to their teacher or supervisor instead of delivering a presentation in person.

An outgoing person—

A) is unlikely to be friendly with a shy person

B) is more likely to get a job than a shy person

C) is more likely to deliver a presentation than to write a report

D) is more likely to finish his or her work on time than a shy person

13. Many people enjoy the independence of owning and driving their own cars, but car ownership and commuting can become very expensive. In addition, driving in traffic is stressful and time-consuming. In order to save time and money, many people get to work or complete their daily tasks by carpooling, or sharing cars with their friends and co-workers. People take turns driving to work and other destinations, sharing the ride with their friends. This way, they can share fuel costs. Also, there is less traffic since there are fewer cars on the road.

The author of this passage probably assumes that:

A) Traffic problems are not important to many people.

B) It is hard for people to organize their schedules in order to carpool.

C) Carpooling is a bad idea.

D) Carpooling is a good idea.

14. Many people love going into a store to do their shopping—trying on clothes, examining fruit, vegetables, and other goods, or talking to salespeople. However, more and more people do their shopping on the Internet. Online shopping saves time and is incredibly convenient; a variety of products are available at the click of a button. One drawback, however, is the cost of shipping. Store customers can bring their purchases home on the same day; online shoppers, however, must pay for shipping and wait for their purchases to be delivered.

    *Drawback* means:

    **A)** problem

    **B)** drawing

    **C)** cost

    **D)** expense

15. Nocturnal animals are animals that sleep during the day and are active at night. They may search for food, hunt, breed, fight, play, or do any other activity throughout the night, returning to their nests or lairs at sunrise to rest until sundown, when they come out again. Nocturnal animals are found throughout the United States and Canada and include bats, owls, certain species of cats, foxes, raccoons, possums, and more.

    What can the reader conclude from this passage?

    **A)** There are not many types of nocturnal animals.

    **B)** Nocturnal animals are relatively common.

    **C)** Nocturnal animals are relatively uncommon.

    **D)** Nocturnal animals are only found in the United States and Canada.

16. Niagara Falls is a popular destination for tourists. In the summer, tourists can take boats around the spectacular waterfall, and they can spend time exploring the local regions of upstate New York and southern Ontario. The city of Toronto is not far away. During the winter, sometimes the falls freeze over into enormous frozen icicles, amazing visitors. The falls rest right on the border between the United States and Canada, so tourists must remember to bring their passports if they wish to take advantage of all the attractions the region has to offer.

    According to the passage, Niagara Falls—

    **A)** is closed in the winter because it is frozen

    **B)** is only open in the summer because that is when tourists can visit it by boat

    **C)** is part of a larger region that is of interest to tourists

    **D)** is located in Canada

17. Chicago is the third-largest city in the United States. Located on the shores of Lake Michigan, Chicago is home to the Willis Tower, the tallest building in the U.S.; the Art Institute of Chicago, with world-renowned exhibitions; and Wrigley Field, home of the popular (if unlucky) Chicago Cubs, one of America's most famous baseball teams. Chicagoans enjoy cuisines from around the world. And, of course, any given night of the week music lovers can find great jazz and blues performers in the many clubs in this center of American music.

    It can be concluded from this passage that:

    **A)** Chicago is an interesting place to live and visit.

    **B)** It is difficult to find classical music concerts in Chicago.

    **C)** The Chicago Cubs will soon win the World Series.

    **D)** Jazz and blues are only played well in Chicago.

CONTINUE →

# ESL – Sentence Meaning

*Complete the sentence with the correct word or phrase.*

1. During the 1950s, rock and roll music _____ very popular.

   **A)** become

   **B)** becoming

   **C)** became

   **D)** had became

2. Mai was _____ to her vacation.

   **A)** looking forward

   **B)** looking though

   **C)** looking at

   **D)** looking towards

3. Even though she is the _____ employee, Jessi finishes more projects than anyone else in the office.

   **A)** most new

   **B)** newer

   **C)** most newest

   **D)** newest

4. With majestic mountains, rolling prairies, breathtaking coastlines, and arctic expanses, the Canadian landscape _____ around the world for its beauty and diversity.

   **A)** are famous

   **B)** is famous

   **C)** famous

   **D)** were famous

5. Despite studying for hours, Carlos could not _____ the math assignment.

   **A)** figure out

   **B)** figure on

   **C)** figure around

   **D)** figure through

6. The children did not want to _____ their room after playing with all their toys.

   **A)** clean up

   **B)** clean over

   **C)** clear around

   **D)** clean off

7. Shawna is _____ than Alyssa at soccer, but Alyssa is a great basketball player.

   **A)** more good

   **B)** more better

   **C)** better

   **D)** the best

8. The water company plans to build a new pipe to bring water _____ the community, improving the service.

   **A)** from

   **B)** out of

   **C)** to

   **D)** on

*Read the sentence(s), then answer the question.*

9. The two men did not see eye to eye on how to finish the project.

   How did the men feel about the project?

   **A)** They agreed on how to finish it.

   **B)** They did not agree on how to finish it.

   **C)** They did not know how to finish it.

   **D)** They did not want to finish it.

10. Nadia had a good excuse for being late to class, so the teacher gave her the benefit of the doubt.

    How did the teacher feel about Nadia and her reason for being late?

    **A)** He was annoyed.

    **B)** He was confused.

    **C)** He did not trust her.

    **D)** He believed her.

11. The marble base gave the object a sense of permanence.

It seemed like the object would—

A) be there forever

B) be there for a short time

C) soon disappear

D) quickly fall over

12. Mrs. Gonzalez wouldn't be caught dead without her makeup on.

Mrs. Gonzalez—

A) will never die wearing her makeup

B) would never be seen without wearing makeup

C) would die before wearing makeup outside

D) is allergic to makeup

13. After a long day of work, Roger wanted to hit the sack.

Roger wanted to—

A) hit a bag

B) sit down

C) go to bed

D) put down his bag

14. Tyrese couldn't wait for his party.

Tyrese—

A) was very excited for his party

B) was too busy to have a party

C) had more important things to do than have a party

D) thought his party was planned too far in advance

15. Ron has two jobs, begins work at seven o'clock in the morning, and also takes classes online.

Which best describes Ron?

A) boring

B) caring

C) studious

D) hardworking

16. After their wedding, it looked like nothing but blue skies ahead for Sofia and Daniel.

Sofia and Daniel—

A) expected nice weather after their wedding

B) expected a positive future after their wedding

C) did not expect nice weather after their wedding

D) did not expect a positive future after their wedding

17. Christine and Daniella enjoy dancing, going to clubs, and parties.

Which best describes Christine and Daniella?

A) busy

B) fun-loving

C) friendly

D) lazy

18. Florida is a great place for a vacation: with family attractions, beautiful beaches, many flights from within the U.S., and reasonable hotels, it offers the best of both worlds.

Florida is a good place for a vacation because:

A) It is good for families and single people.

B) It has fun activities for children and adults.

C) It has all the advantages of an ideal destination.

D) It has two fun things to do.

19. Nicolas and Alexander had been friends for many years; their relationship was rock-solid.

Which best describes the boys' friendship?

A) It was very strong.

B) It was rocky.

C) It was at risk.

D) It was rigorous.

→ CONTINUE

**20.** Janice does not beat around the bush at work, so her boss assigns her the most urgent projects.

Janice—

A) rushes through her work

B) works too quickly

C) does not work well with others

D) does not waste time at work

**21.** Rita always chooses what restaurant to visit with her friends—she will even try to order their food for them.

Rita is—

A) knowledgeable

B) bossy

C) friendly

D) outgoing

# ANSWER KEY

## Arithmetic

| | | | | | | | |
|---|---|---|---|---|---|---|---|
| 1. | A) | 6. | D) | 11. | A) | 16. | C) |
| 2. | B) | 7. | C) | 12. | B) | 17. | D) |
| 3. | C) | 8. | A) | 13. | D) | | |
| 4. | C) | 9. | C) | 14. | B) | | |
| 5. | D) | 10. | C) | 15. | B) | | |

## Elementary Algebra

| | | | | | | | |
|---|---|---|---|---|---|---|---|
| 1. | D) | 4. | C) | 7. | D) | 10. | B) |
| 2. | C) | 5. | C) | 8. | B) | 11. | A) |
| 3. | C) | 6. | A) | 9. | C) | 12. | A) |

## College-Level Math

| | | | | | | | |
|---|---|---|---|---|---|---|---|
| 1. | B) | 6. | E) | 11. | A) | 16. | B) |
| 2. | B) | 7. | C) | 12. | E) | 17. | C) |
| 3. | A) | 8. | D) | 13. | B) | 18. | C) |
| 4. | C) | 9. | A) | 14. | C) | 19. | D) |
| 5. | E) | 10. | D) | 15. | B) | 20. | C) |

## Reading Comprehension

| | | | | | | | |
|---|---|---|---|---|---|---|---|
| 1. | B) | 7. | B) | 13. | A) | 19. | B) |
| 2. | D) | 8. | C) | 14. | C) | 20. | C) |
| 3. | C) | 9. | A) | 15. | B) | 21. | A) |
| 4. | D) | 10. | A) | 16. | D) | 22. | A) |
| 5. | B) | 11. | B) | 17. | C) | | |
| 6. | D) | 12. | C) | 18. | D) | | |

## Sentence Skills

| | | | | | | | |
|---|---|---|---|---|---|---|---|
| 1. | D) | 8. | B) | 15. | C) | 22. | B) |
| 2. | C) | 9. | C) | 16. | A) | 23. | B) |
| 3. | B) | 10. | B) | 17. | A) | 24. | C) |
| 4. | C) | 11. | A) | 18. | A) | 25. | C) |
| 5. | A) | 12. | B) | 19. | B) | | |
| 6. | D) | 13. | A) | 20. | D) | | |
| 7. | D) | 14. | D) | 21. | B) | | |

## ESL – Language Use

| | | | | | | | |
|---|---|---|---|---|---|---|---|
| 1. | B) | 6. | B) | 11. | B) | 16. | C) |
| 2. | D) | 7. | C) | 12. | D) | 17. | D) |
| 3. | C) | 8. | B) | 13. | A) | 18. | C) |
| 4. | D) | 9. | A) | 14. | B) | | |
| 5. | D) | 10. | D) | 15. | B) | | |

## ESL – Reading Skills

| | | | | | | | |
|---|---|---|---|---|---|---|---|
| 1. | B) | 6. | A) | 11. | B) | 16. | C) |
| 2. | A) | 7. | D) | 12. | C) | 17. | A) |
| 3. | A) | 8. | B) | 13. | D) | | |
| 4. | C) | 9. | D) | 14. | A) | | |
| 5. | C) | 10. | A) | 15. | B) | | |

## ESL – Sentence Meaning

| | | | | | | | |
|---|---|---|---|---|---|---|---|
| 1. | C) | 7. | C) | 13. | C) | 19. | A) |
| 2. | A) | 8. | C) | 14. | A) | 20. | D) |
| 3. | D) | 9. | B) | 15. | D) | 21. | B) |
| 4. | B) | 10. | D) | 16. | B) | | |
| 5. | A) | 11. | A) | 17. | B) | | |
| 6. | A) | 12. | B) | 18. | C) | | |

# 8

# PRACTICE TEST TWO

## ARITHMETIC

**1.** If the value of y is between 0.0047 and 0.0162, which of the following could be y?

    **A)** 0.0035

    **B)** 0.0055

    **C)** 0.0185

    **D)** 0.0238

**2.** $4\frac{1}{2} - 1\frac{2}{3} =$

    **A)** $2\frac{1}{3}$

    **B)** $2\frac{5}{6}$

    **C)** $3\frac{1}{6}$

    **D)** $3\frac{5}{6}$

**3.** $59.09 - 5.007 - 6.21 =$

    **A)** 47.792

    **B)** 47.81

    **C)** 47.873

    **D)** 47.882

**4.** 7 is what percent of 60?

    **A)** 4.20

    **B)** 8.57

    **C)** 10.11

    **D)** 11.67

**5.** $0.08 \times 0.12 =$

    **A)** 0.0096

    **B)** 0.096

    **C)** 0.96

    **D)** 9.6

**6.** Tiles are $12.51 per square yard. What will it cost to tile a room with if the room is 10 feet wide and 12 feet long?

    **A)** $166.80

    **B)** $178.70

    **C)** $184.60

    **D)** $190.90

**7.** $10\frac{3}{8} \div \frac{1}{3} =$

    **A)** $3\frac{13}{24}$

    **B)** $6\frac{3}{4}$

    **C)** $15\frac{3}{4}$

    **D)** $31\frac{1}{8}$

8. A car dealership has sedans, SUVs, and minivans in a ratio of 6:3:1, respectively. What proportion of the vehicles at the dealership are sedans?

   A) $\frac{1}{6}$

   B) $\frac{3}{10}$

   C) $\frac{1}{2}$

   D) $\frac{3}{5}$

9. If there are 380 female students in a class, and male students make up 60% of the class, how many total students are in the class?

   A) 570

   B) 633

   C) 950

   D) 2280

10. $4 - \frac{1}{2^2} + 24 \div (8 + 12) =$

    A) 1.39

    B) 2.74

    C) 4.95

    D) 15.28

11. Dora commutes to work every day. During the week, her commute times were 29.15 minutes, 30.75 minutes, 28.59 minutes, 27.20 minutes, and 35.62 minutes. If the times are rounded to nearest minute, which is the best estimate of the total time Dora spent on her commute during this week?

    A) 149

    B) 150

    C) 151

    D) 152

12. What is 18 percent of 11,400?

    A) 633

    B) 2052

    C) 3553

    D) 8700

13. What is $\frac{1587}{98}$ rounded to the nearest integer?

    A) 15

    B) 16

    C) 17

    D) 18

14. A marinade recipe calls for 2 tablespoons of lemon juice for $\frac{1}{4}$ cup of olive oil. How many tablespoons of lemon juice would be used with $\frac{2}{3}$ cup olive oil?

    A) $\frac{3}{4}$

    B) $2\frac{1}{3}$

    C) 4

    D) $5\frac{1}{3}$

15. How many digits are in the sum $951.4 + 98.908 + 1.053$?

    A) 4

    B) 5

    C) 6

    D) 7

16. $105.71 \div 31 =$

    A) 0.341

    B) 3.41

    C) 34.1

    D) 341

17. Which of the following is the least?

    A) 1.068

    B) 1.680

    C) 1.608

    D) 1.086

# ELEMENTARY ALGEBRA

1. Which expression is equivalent to
   $2(-3x - 2) < 2$?

   A) $x > -2$

   B) $x < -\frac{2}{3}$

   C) $x < -1$

   D) $x > -1$

2. $x^3 - 3x^2 + (2x)^3 - x =$

   A) $20x$

   B) $x^3 - 3x^2 + 7x$

   C) $7x^3 - 3x^2 - x$

   D) $9x^3 - 3x^2 - x$

3. What is the value of the expression $\frac{4x}{x-1}$ when
   $x = 5$?

   A) 3

   B) 4

   C) 5

   D) 6

4. If $3a + 4 = 2a$, then $a = ?$

   A) $-4$

   B) $-\frac{4}{5}$

   C) $\frac{4}{5}$

   D) 4

5. Which of the following lists of numbers is in
   order from least to greatest?

   A) $\frac{1}{24} < \frac{3}{32} < \frac{5}{48} < \frac{2}{16} < \frac{3}{16}$

   B) $\frac{1}{24} < \frac{5}{48} < \frac{3}{32} < \frac{2}{16} < \frac{3}{16}$

   C) $\frac{1}{24} < \frac{3}{32} < \frac{2}{16} < \frac{3}{16} < \frac{5}{48}$

   D) $\frac{1}{24} < \frac{2}{16} < \frac{3}{32} < \frac{3}{16} < \frac{5}{48}$

6. A cleaning company charges $25 per hour
   per room. A 7% sales tax is added to this
   charge. If $t$ represents the number of hours
   and $r$ represents the number of rooms,
   which of the following algebraic equations
   represents the total cost $c$ of cleaning?

   A) $c = 25.07(t)(r)$

   B) $c = 32.00(t)(r)$

   C) $c = 26.75(t)(r)$

   D) $c = \frac{26.75(t)}{(r)}$

7. For which of the following expressions are $x =$
   3 and $x = -2$ both solutions?

   A) $x^2 - x - 6$

   B) $x^2 - x + 6$

   C) $x^2 + x - 6$

   D) $x^2 + x + 6$

8. $100x^2 + 25x =$

   A) $25(4x + x)$

   B) $25(4x^2 + x)$

   C) $25x(4x + 1)$

   D) $100x(x + 25x)$

9. If $m$ represents a car's average mileage in
   miles per gallon, $p$ represents the price of
   gas in dollars per gallon, and $d$ represents
   a distance in miles, which of the following
   algebraic equations represents the cost ($c$) of
   gas per mile?

   A) $c = \frac{dp}{m}$

   B) $c = \frac{p}{m}$

   C) $c = \frac{mp}{d}$

   D) $c = \frac{m}{p}$

10. If $y = |x - 28|$, what is the value of $y$ when
    $x = 12$?

    A) $-40$

    B) $-16$

    C) 16

    D) 40

**11.** Melissa is ordering fencing to enclose an area of 5625 square feet in the shape of a square. How many feet of fencing does she need?

   **A)** 75

   **B)** 150

   **C)** 300

   **D)** 5,625

**12.** $\frac{21x^4 + 14x^2}{7x} =$

   **A)** $3x^3 + 2x$

   **B)** $3x^5 + 2x^3$

   **C)** $\frac{3x^4 + 2x}{x}$

   **D)** $\frac{3x^3 + 2x}{7}$

# COLLEGE-LEVEL MATH

1. Sequence $\{a_n\}$ is defined as $a_n = 11, 7, 3, -1, \ldots$ where $a_1 = 11$. Which expression defines $a_n$?

   A) $a_n = 11 + 4(n - 1)$

   B) $a_n = 11(4)^{(n-1)}$

   C) $a_n = 11 - 4n$

   D) $a_n = 15 - 4n$

   E) $a_n = 15 + 4(n - 1)$

2. $3a^2 - 11a + 10 = 0$

   What is the sum of all the values of $a$ that satisfy the equation above?

   A) 3

   B) 7

   C) 13

   D) 15

   E) 30

3. For which of the following functions does $f(x) = |f(x)|$ for every value of $x$?

   A) $f(x) = x^{\frac{1}{3}}$

   B) $f(x) = 3 - x$

   C) $f(x) = 2x + x^2$

   D) $f(x) = x^3 + 1$

   E) $f(x) = x^2 + (2 - x)^2$

4. If $f(x) = 3^x - 2$, what is the value of $f(5)$?

   A) 13

   B) 27

   C) 241

   D) 243

   E) 727

5. $|3x - 5| = 23$

   $|10 + 4y| = 12$

   If $x$ and $y$ are both negative numbers in the system of equations above, what is $|y - x|$?

   A) 0.5

   B) 4

   C) 7.33

   D) 8

   E) 8.5

6. If $y = \log_x 64$, what is the value of $y$ when $x = 4$?

   A) $\frac{1}{2}$

   B) $\frac{1}{3}$

   C) 2

   D) 3

   E) 16

7. A root of $x^2 + 7x = -8$ is

   A) $-8$

   B) $-7 + \sqrt{\frac{17}{2}}$

   C) $-7 + \sqrt{\frac{41}{2}}$

   D) 1

   E) $7 - \sqrt{\frac{17}{2}}$

8. If $f(x) = 8x + 2$ and $g(x) = x + \frac{6}{8}$, then $f(g(x)) =$

   A) $x + 1$

   B) $x + 8$

   C) $x + 6$

   D) $8x + 8$

   E) $8x + 50$

9. A radio station plays songs that last an average of 3.5 minutes and has commercial breaks that last 2 minutes. If the station is required to play 1 commercial break for every 4 songs, how many songs can the station play in an hour?

   A) 14

   B) 15

   C) 16

   D) 17

   E) 18

10. If $\frac{x}{7} = x - 36$, then $\left(\frac{x}{2}\right)^2 =$

    A) 5.0625

    B) 9

    C) 441

    D) 20,736

    E) 15,876

11. What is the surface area of a box that is 12 inches long, 18 inches wide, and 6 inches high?

A) 144 in²

B) 396 in²

C) 412 in²

D) 792 in²

E) 1,296 in²

12. The graph of which of the following equations is a straight line perpendicular to the graph of $y = 2.5x - 3$?

A) $y = -0.4 + 2.5$

B) $y = -2.5 + 0.4$

C) $y = 0.33 + 0.4$

D) $y = 0.33 + .04$

E) $y = 0.4 + 2.5$

13. Out of 7 students, 3 will be chosen to represent the school at a city council meeting. How many different groups of 3 students can be chosen?

A) 21

B) 27

C) 35

D) 210

E) 343

14. The area of a right triangle is 24.5 square centimeters. If one of its angles measures 45°, what is the length of its hypotenuse in centimeters?

A) 7

B) 8.9

C) 9.9

D) 10

E) 17.3

15. $(5 + \sqrt{5})(5 - \sqrt{5})=$

A) $10\sqrt{5}$

B) 20

C) 25

D) $25\sqrt{5}$

E) $25 - 2\sqrt{5}$

16. A painting is leaning against a wall. If the painting is 20 inches tall and forms a 20° angle with the wall, how many inches is the base of the painting from the wall?

A) 6.8

B) 7.3

C) 8.2

D) 18.8

E) 58.5

17. A circle and line are plotted on the same coordinate plane. What is the maximum number of points at which the circle and line can intersect?

A) 0

B) 1

C) 2

D) 3

E) More than 3

18. A chemical experiment requires that a solute be diluted with 4 parts (by mass) water for every 1 part (by mass) solute. If the desired mass for the solution is 90 grams, how many grams of solute should be used?

A) 15

B) 16.5

C) 18

D) 22.5

E) 72

19. $3a(4a + 6) - (2a - 4) =$

A) $-(12a + 1)(a + 1)$

B) $(12a - 1)(a - 1)$

C) $(12a + 4)(a - 1)$

D) $(12a - 4)(a + 1)$

E) $(12a + 4)(a + 1)$

20. If $x^2 - 9 < 0$, what are all the possible values of $x$?

A) $x > 3$ or $x < -3$

B) $-3 < x < 3$

C) $x > 3$

D) $x < -3$

E) $x < 9$

# READING COMPREHENSION

*Directions for questions 1 – 12: Read the passage. Then choose the best answer to the question based on what you read.*

1. For centuries China stood as a leading civilization, outpacing the rest of the world in the arts and sciences, but in the nineteenth and early twentieth centuries, the country was beset by civil unrest, major famines, military defeats, and foreign occupation. After World War II, the communists under Mao Zedong established an autocratic socialist system that, while ensuring China's sovereignty, imposed strict controls over everyday life and cost the lives of tens of millions of people. After 1978, Mao's successor Deng Xiaoping and other leaders focused on market-oriented economic development and by 2000 output had quadrupled. For much of the population, living standards have improved dramatically and the room for personal choice has expanded, yet political controls remain tight. Since the early 1990s, China has increased its global outreach and participation in international organizations.

    *Courtesy CIA World Factbook, 2015*

    Following the rule of Mao Zedong, China's economy—

    A) faltered due to continuing tight political controls

    B) developed rapidly after moving to a market-based model

    C) developed into an autocratic socialist system that imposed strict controls over everyday life

    D) helped the country become a leading global civilization

2. Providing students with their own laptop or tablet will allow them to explore new programs and software in class with teachers and classmates and to practice using it at home. In schools without laptops for students, classes have to visit computer labs where they share old computers often missing keys or that run so slowly they are hardly powered on before class ends. When a teacher tries to show students how to use a new tool or website, students must scramble to follow along and have no time to explore the new feature. If they can take laptops home instead, students can do things like practice editing video clips or photographs until they are perfect. They can email classmates or use shared files to collaborate even after school. If schools expect students to learn these skills, it is the schools' responsibility to provide students with enough opportunities to practice them.

    The author's purpose in writing this passage is to

    A) teach high school students how to use computers properly.

    B) describe the ways that schools make technology available to students today.

    C) argue that schools should make computer technology available to students.

    D) illustrate the benefits of technology in academics.

3. The Americas were quickly colonized by Europeans after Christopher Columbus first laid claim to them for the Spanish, and the British, French and Spanish all held territories in North America throughout the sixteenth, seventeenth, eighteenth and nineteenth centuries. The British ultimately controlled most of the

    Atlantic coast and some territories inland—what became known as the Thirteen Colonies—while France controlled most of what is today Quebec, the Midwest, and the Mississippi River Valley region. Spain's holdings extended through Mexico into Texas, the Southwest, and eventually California, reaching as far north into what are today parts of Montana and Wyoming, in addition to Florida. The Northeast and

    Upper Midwest were rich in game and beaver pelts, and the areas on the mid-Atlantic coast were agriculturally fertile. They also contained important commercial centers like New York, Boston and Philadelphia where North American products went to port.

    It could be concluded from this passage that European powers were interested in colonizing North America because

CONTINUE

**A)** North America was rich in land and profitable natural resources; furthermore, coastal settlements allowed these products to be easily shipped overseas.

**B)** France and Britain wanted to compete with Spain for resources in the Western Hemisphere.

**C)** Christopher Columbus' initial voyages made it safer for other explorers to lay claim to inland territory.

**D)** the large amount of land made it possible for Britain, France and Spain to split territory equitably.

4. Meteorologists study the climate of an area, its typical weather pattern over an extended period of time. For example, much of the United States experiences a four-season cycle, or temperate climate, while Central Africa, Southeast Asia and parts of Central and South America (located between the Tropic of Cancer and the Tropic of Capricorn) have tropical climates, characterized by high humidity. Climates can determine the nature of land: a desert is an area where there is little precipitation, or rain, resulting in limited vegetation and infertile land. In the hydrologic cycle, water circulates between the land, the atmosphere, and the hydrosphere, or bodies of water on the Earth. Storms like hurricanes, found in the tropical West Atlantic Ocean and the Caribbean Sea, typhoons, in the western Pacific, and cyclones in the Indian Ocean, are all major storms with winds that reach speeds of at least seventy-four miles per hour.

Major storms like hurricanes, typhoons and cyclones are distinguished by

**A)** appearing as part of the hydrologic cycle.

**B)** winds with speeds of at least seventy-five miles per hour.

**C)** winds with speeds of at least seventy-four miles per hour.

**D)** winds with speeds up to seventy-four miles per hour.

5. Major tenets of Hindu belief include reincarnation, or that the universe and its beings undergo endless cycles of rebirth and karma, that one creates one's own destiny. The soul is reincarnated until it has resolved all karmas, at which point it attains moksha, or liberation from the cycle. Hindus believe in multiple divine beings. The religion is based in the Vedic scriptures; other important texts include the Upanishads, the Mahabharata, and the Bhagavad Gita. Hinduism is the primary religion in India and is intertwined with the caste system, the hierarchical societal structure.

The purpose of this passage is to present

**A)** a comparison of Hindu religion and social structure.

**B)** a description of reincarnation.

**C)** a listing of important Hindu literature.

**D)** a brief overview of Hinduism and its main precepts.

6. It's easy to puzzle over the landscapes of our solar system's distant planets—how could we ever know what those far-flung places really look like? However, scientists utilize a number of tools to visualize the surfaces of many planets. The topography of Venus, for example, has been explored by several space probes, including the Russian Venera landers and NASA's Magellan orbiter. These craft used imaging and radar to map the surface of the planet, identifying a whole host of features including volcanoes, craters, and a complex system of channels. Mars has likewise been mapped by space probes, including the famous Mars Rovers, which are automated vehicles that actually landed on the planet's surface. These rovers have been used by NASA and other space agencies to study the geology, climate, and possible biology of the planet.

In addition to these long-range probes, NASA has also used its series of orbiting telescopes to study distant planets. These four massively powerful telescopes include the famous Hubble Space Telescope as well as the Compton Gamma Ray Observatory, Chandra X-Ray Observatory, and the Spitzer Space Telescope. These allow scientists to examine planets using not only visible light but also infrared and near-infrared light, ultraviolet light, x-rays and gamma rays.

Powerful telescopes aren't just found in space: NASA makes use of Earth-bound telescopes as well. Scientists at the National Radio Astronomy Observatory in Charlottesville, VA, have spent decades using radio imaging to build an incredibly detailed portrait of Venus' surface. In fact, Earth-bound telescopes offer a distinct advantage over orbiting telescopes because they allow scientists to capture data from a fixed point, which in turn allows them to effectively compare data collected over long period of time.

Which of the following sentences best describes the main idea of the passage?

**A)** It's impossible to know what the surfaces of other planets are really like.

**B)** Telescopes are an important tool for scientists studying planets in our solar system.

**C)** Venus' surface has many of the same features as the Earth's, including volcanoes, craters, and channels.

**D)** Scientists use a variety of advanced technologies to study the surface of the planets in our solar system.

7. The U.S. Constitution is a single document codifying the foundational laws of the country. It provides for a federal government, but one that is based on popular sovereignty, separation of powers, limited government and checks and balances in order to protect from federal overreach. Popular sovereignty meant that government can only exist with the consent of the governed. One important example of protection of that consent in the Constitution is habeas corpus, according to which the government cannot detain a person indefinitely without charges. The three articles of the Constitution laid out a framework for a limited federal government, including a separation of powers between the legislative (Article I), executive (Article II), and judicial (Article III) branches. Each of these branches has the ability to check, or limit, the powers of the others. Powers held by more than one branch of government are called concurrent powers.

The purpose of the three branches of government is to

**A)** ensure that each branch of government is limited in its powers by the other two—a system of checks and balances.

**B)** ensure that each branch of government is limited in its powers by the other two—a system of popular sovereignty.

**C)** ensure that government can only exist with the consent of the governed.

**D)** protect the rule of habeas corpus.

8. Exercise is critical for healthy development in children. Today, there is an epidemic of unhealthy children in the United States who will face health problems in adulthood due to poor diet and lack of exercise in childhood. This is a problem for all Americans, especially with the rising cost of healthcare.

It is vital that school systems and parents encourage their children to engage in a minimum of thirty minutes of cardiovascular exercise each day, mildly increasing their heart rate for a sustained period. This is proven to decrease the likelihood of developmental diabetes, obesity, and a multitude of other health problems. Also, children need a proper diet rich in fruits and vegetables so that they can grow and develop physically, as well as learn healthy eating habits early on.

Parents and schools are responsible for

**A)** covering the rising cost of healthcare in the United States today.

**B)** getting thirty minutes of cardiovascular exercise per day and eating nutritious meals.

**C)** decreasing the likelihood of developmental diabetes, obesity, and other problems.

**D)** ensuring that children get at least thirty minutes of exercise per day and receive nutritious meals.

9. The issue of public transportation has begun to haunt the fast-growing cities of the southern United States. Cities like Atlanta, Dallas, and Houston are full of sprawling suburbs and single-family homes, not densely concentrated skyscrapers and apartments. Highways are the twenty-lane-wide expanses of concrete that allow commuters to move from home to work and back again. But these modern miracles have become time-sucking, pollution-spewing nightmares. It's time for these cities to adopt public transport like trains and buses if they are to remain livable.

This passage implies that

CONTINUE

**A)** cities in the southern United States are growing more rapidly than anywhere else in the nation.

**B)** public transportation is too difficult to integrate into cities like Atlanta, Dallas, and Houston, which are dependent on cars and highways.

**C)** Atlanta, Dallas and Houston do not currently have strong public transportation systems.

**D)** highways are modern miracles.

10. The explorations of European sailors and their patrons in the fifteenth century were not the result of a desire to discover new lands, but rather to discover better trade routes and spread European culture and the Christian religion. They were, at this time, particularly interested in South and East Asia, relatively untouched by earlier Christian missionaries and difficult to access for traders. The desire to convert new Christians was especially pressing for the Catholic Church in the face of the Protestant Reformation, which began at the very end of the fifteenth century.

According to the passage, European exploration in the fifteenth century focused on

**A)** the discovery of new lands, such as those found in the Western Hemisphere.

**B)** spreading the Protestant Reformation.

**C)** finding better trade routes and spreading Christianity.

**D)** finding better trade routes only.

11. A land of vast distances and rich natural resources, Canada became a self-governing dominion in 1867, while retaining ties to the British crown. Economically and technologically, the nation has developed in parallel with the US, its neighbor to the south across the world's longest unfortified border. Canada faces the political challenges of meeting public demands for quality improvements in health care, education, social services, and economic competitiveness, as well as responding to the particular concerns of predominantly francophone Quebec. Canada also aims to develop its diverse energy resources while maintaining its commitment to the environment.

*Courtesy CIA World Factbook 2015*

The passage implies that

**A)** Canada remains under the control of Great Britain.

**B)** Canada and the United States have a strong and positive relationship.

**C)** Canada has developed thanks to support from the United States.

**D)** Canada is unable to meet many of the political challenges with which it is faced.

12. Language branches are built on actual, documented languages that evolved from an ancient ancestor language no longer spoken today. Latin is the basis of a language branch. You may, for instance, find it relatively easy to understand Italian if you can speak Spanish, because they are both based in Latin, the now-dead language of the Roman Empire; however, but they are distinct languages with their own rules, grammar and vocabulary.

A language group encompasses all the living languages that are part of a language branch. The languages that evolved out of Latin, including Spanish and Italian, are called the Romance languages. The individual languages have their own dialects and accents. Similar languages may share some vocabulary or grammar; while some words or usages may differ, if you can speak a language, you can understand a regional dialect (perhaps with some difficulty).

The purpose of this passage is to explain

**A)** the technical methods linguists use to organize and classify languages.

**B)** how languages are related based on the ancestry they share.

**C)** why Spanish and Italian sound similar.

**D)** why a Spanish-speaking person can learn Italian easily.

*Directions for questions 13 – 22: Two sentences are shown and then followed by a question or a statement. Determine the best answer to the question or the best way to complete the statement.*

13. High heat and humidity can trigger asthma attacks in children and the elderly.

    Providing air conditioning can significantly reduce the risk of asthma attacks in these vulnerable populations during hot and humid days; recent studies have proved this in Louisiana and Florida.

    What does the underlined sentence do?

    A) It states an effect.

    B) It proposes a solution.

    C) It gives an example.

    D) It analyzes the statement made in the first.

14. Alligators look heavy and slow, but they can move very quickly; in Florida and the Gulf Coast of the United States, it is important to be cautious in areas where alligators live.

    There are increasing reports of alligators being discovered in homeowners' backyards as housing developments expand into alligator habitats; upsetting stories of alligator attacks on pets are not unheard of.

    What does the underlined sentence do?

    A) It makes a contrast.

    B) It expands on the first sentence.

    C) It states an effect.

    D) It reinforces the first.

15. Mountain climbing is a popular sport around the world; thanks to expeditionary companies, more people than ever before are able to try to climb the highest mountains on every continent and enjoy this exciting activity.

    Mountain climbing is a popular but risky sport; untrained climbers pose a risk to themselves and to others when they try to climb peaks that are too difficult for them, and expeditionary companies act unprofessionally when they encourage this.

What does the underlined sentence do?

A) It reinforces the first.

B) It proposes a solution.

C) It analyzes a statement made in the first.

D) It makes a contrast.

16. The Voting Rights Act of 1965 helped ensure that states would not be able to enforce regulations that inhibited certain people—mainly African Americans—from voting.

    More African Americans in the South—many of whom had survived living under segregation—were finally able to exercise their right to vote as a result of this Act.

    What does the underlined sentence do?

    A) It states an effect.

    B) It provides an example.

    C) It proposes a solution.

    D) It expands on the first sentence.

17. Learning to play a musical instrument is very popular in many schools, and students are encouraged from a young age to study the piano, violin, flute, or to join the school orchestra.

    Today, musical study is discouraged more than ever in the United States due to budget cuts for the arts, but many argue that it is more important to spend money on supplementary math and science teaching instead.

    What does the underlined sentence do?

    A) It draws a conclusion about what is stated in the first.

    B) It makes a contrast.

    C) It contradicts the first.

    D) It proposes a solution.

18. Beekeeping is a useful skill for anyone interested in serious gardening, for bees are essential in pollination and can help maintain healthy plants and flowers.

    When one community garden added an apiary, the garden produced twice as many fruits and vegetables than it had the year before, and the flowers were larger and brighter.

What does the underlined sentence do?

**A)** It provides an example.

**B)** It analyzes a statement in the first sentence.

**C)** It makes a contrast.

**D)** It expands on the first sentence.

19. Flash mobs, or groups of people organized on social media who seemingly randomly appear in public to engage in rambunctious behavior, are an amusing, but harmless, social phenomenon.

    While some find it fun to be part of a flash mob, the same cannot be said for those regular people going about their business only to be interrupted by the annoying antics of the flash mob as it descends upon a busy street corner.

    How do the two sentences relate?

    **A)** They contradict each other.

    **B)** They present a contrast.

    **C)** They present a problem and a solution.

    **D)** They express roughly the same idea.

20. Many people enjoy a cup of strong coffee in the morning, but some prefer tea due to its lower caffeine content; caffeine can cause tension and "jitters."

    Tea contains less coffee than caffeine, which many consumers find preferable, particularly if they suffer from anxiety or high blood pressure.

    How do the two sentences relate?

    **A)** They establish a contrast.

    **B)** They present a contradiction.

    **C)** They reinforce each other.

    **D)** They present an argument followed by an example.

21. Scuba diving is a popular pastime for tourists at tropical resorts; however, this activity can threaten the fragile ecosystems of the underwater reefs which divers wish to explore.

    Many diving companies now offer educational courses and training to help educate scuba divers learn to safely navigate the beautiful underwater landscapes they wish to visit without disturbing the wildlife.

    How do the two sentences relate?

    **A)** They present a problem and a solution.

    **B)** They reinforce each other.

    **C)** They express roughly the same idea.

    **D)** They present a contradiction.

22. Many young college graduates move to major cities like New York, Los Angeles, and Chicago after finishing school in order to pursue careers in business, the arts, social justice, and other professions; these cities offer abundant opportunities in these fields.

    Despite the myriad opportunities in major American cities for recent graduates seeking professional careers, the cost of living in urban centers like New York, Chicago, Los Angeles and elsewhere is exorbitant, and many young people leave these areas after a few years.

    What does the second sentence do?

    **A)** It proposes a solution.

    **B)** It states an effect.

    **C)** It makes a contrast.

    **D)** It reinforces the first.

# SENTENCE SKILLS

*Directions for questions 1 – 12: In the following questions, select the answer that best rewrites the underlined portion of the sentence. Note that the first answer choice indicates no change was made to the sentence.*

1. To horseback ride, surf, and rock climb are Terrence's favorite activities.

   A) To horseback ride, surf, and rock climb
   B) To horseback riding, surfing, and rock climbing
   C) Horseback ride, surf, and rock climb
   D) Horseback riding, surfing, and rock climbing

2. When puffing out the neck, this is a courtship ritual for the anole lizard.

   A) When puffing out the neck, this
   B) Lizards puff out their necks, this
   C) Puffing out the neck
   D) The fact that lizards puff out their necks

3. Writing daily journal entries, which is an activity meant to improve writing skills and creativity.

   A) entries, which is an activity
   B) entries is an activity because it is
   C) entries, being an activity which is
   D) entries is an activity

4. While staying up late to finish homework, an exam, I remembered, I needed to prepare for the next day.

   A) an exam, I remembered, I needed to prepare for
   B) I remembered I needed to prepare for an exam
   C) an exam I remembered I needed to prepare for
   D) there was an exam, I remembered, for it I needed to prepare

5. For a rat, grinding its teeth together quickly, or chattering, is extremely happy.

   A) For a rat, grinding its teeth
   B) A rat grinding its teeth
   C) When a rat grinds its teeth
   D) To grind its teeth, for a rat

6. Trained all her life, Tatyana set a world record for weight lifting.

   A) Trained all her life,
   B) After training all her life,
   C) To train all her life,
   D) As she trained all her life,

7. To seem like they understand our every word, dogs actually only understand the tone and inflection of human language.

   A) To seem like they understand our every word,
   B) To seem like they understand words,
   C) As it seems like they understand our every word
   D) While it seems like they understand our every word,

8. He was intrigued by the House of Romonov searching for a book about the Russian family.

   A) He was intrigued by the House of Romonov searching
   B) He was intrigued by the House of Romonov searched
   C) Intrigued by the House of Romonov, he searched
   D) The House of Romonov intrigued him, searching

9. Embarrassed, he blushed, and his face turned a bright red.

   A) Embarrassed, he blushed, and his face turned a bright red.
   B) He, embarrassed blushed, and his face
   C) His face was embarrassed, and
   D) His face, he blushed, and

→

CONTINUE

10. Controversial as it was, the author stood by her new book.

    A) Controversial as it was, the author stood by her new book.

    B) The author stood by her new book, controversial as it was.

    C) Controversial, the author, as it was, stood by her new book.

    D) The author stood by her, controversial as it was, new book.

11. The information gathered from the census is used to determine political boundaries and planning transportation systems.

    A) to determine political boundaries and planning transportation systems.

    B) determines political boundaries and plans transportation systems.

    C) to determine political boundaries and planning transportation systems.

    D) to determine political boundaries and plan transportation systems.

12. Many artists and producers disagree over how copyright laws should be applied, they have different perspectives on what best protects and encourages creativity.

    A) should be applied, they have different perspectives

    B) should be applied because they have different perspectives

    C) should apply on differing perspectives

    D) are applied with different perspectives

*Directions for questions 13-25: Select the answer that begins to rewrite the following sentences most effectively and without changing the meaning of the original sentence. Keep in mind that not every answer choice will complete the original sentence.*

13. River otters mate for life, but the same cannot be said of sea otters.

    Rewrite, beginning with:

    *Unlike sea otters,—*

    The next words will be:

    A) the same cannot be said

    B) river otters mate

    C) they don't mate

    D) river otters don't mate

14. While many states have some form of income tax, Texans only pay federal income tax.

    Rewrite, beginning with:

    *Texans only pay federal income tax,—*

    The next words will be:

    A) but many other states have

    B) and many states have

    C) and even though many states

    D) therefore many states have

15. Not only can Mimic octopi change colors, they can mimic the shape and texture of many aquatic animals.

    Rewrite, beginning with:

    *Mimic octopi can mimic the shape and texture of many aquatic animals—*

    The next words will be:

    A) and only change color

    B) but also change color

    C) and change color

    D) only change colors

16. Despite being the founder of Apple, Steve Jobs limited his children's technology usage.

    Rewrite, beginning with:

    *Steve Jobs limited his children's technology usage—*

    The next words will be:

    A) and he was the

    B) even though he was

    C) as he was

    D) therefore he was

17. The actress was astounded when she won the Oscar.

    Rewrite, beginning with:

    *After winning the Oscar,—*

    The next words will be:

    A) astonished.

    B) she was astounded.

    C) feeling astounded

    D) the actress was astounded.

18. The gas prices dropped, and people rushed to the pumps.

Rewrite, beginning with:

*People rushed to the pumps—*

The next words will be:

A) and the gas prices dropped.

B) and then the gas prices dropped.

C) when the gas prices dropped.

D) but the gas prices dropped.

19. After years of paying off loans, Tomas was debt-free.

Rewrite, beginning with:

*Tomas was debt-free—*

The next words will be:

A) having paid off loans for years.

B) paying off loans for years.

C) and paid off loans for years.

D) despite having paying off loans for years.

20. Wolf packs have intricate social groups, similar to humans.

Rewrite, beginning with:

*Like humans,—*

The next words will be:

A) wolf packs have

B) wolf packs do not have

C) having an intricate

D) intricate social groups have

21. The train arrived at the station, and passengers began to disembark.

Rewrite, beginning with:

*Passengers began to disembark—*

The next words will be:

A) and the train arrived

B) before the train arrived

C) after the train arrived

D) even though the train arrived

22. Even though he enjoyed using Facebook and Instagram, Twitter was a different story.

Rewrite, beginning with:

*He didn't enjoy using—*

The next words will be:

A) Instagram despite enjoying

B) Facebook and Twitter because

C) Twitter because he enjoyed

D) Twitter, despite enjoying

23. If the photographer had the equipment, she would experiment with wildlife photography.

Rewrite, beginning with:

*The photographer cannot experiment with wildlife photography—*

The next words will be:

A) when having

B) because she

C) although there

D) with enough

24. Yellow-bellied warblers are often spotted in this community, since they are native to the area.

Rewrite, beginning with:

*Being native to the area,—*

The next words will be:

A) it is common to spot

B) yellow-bellied warblers are often

C) yellow-bellied warblers in this community

D) in this community yellow-bellied warblers are

25. They wrapped sandwiches and bagged chips when they packed for the picnic.

Rewrite, beginning with:

*Packing for the picnic,—*

The next words will be:

A) wrapping sandwiches

B) sandwiches and chips were

C) when they wrapped

D) they wrapped sandwiches

# WRITEPLACER

*Write a multiple-paragraph essay of approximately 300 – 600 words based on the prompt below. Plan, write, review and edit your essay during the time provided, and read the prompt carefully before starting your essay.*

In recent years, powerful storms around the world have caused extreme destruction. However, rapid growth of population and cities has continued in vulnerable areas, putting millions at risk. Supporters of development in these areas say that they are the engines of the economy and must be accommodated to keep economic growth high. Opponents insist that development must be limited in the interest of public safety, even if that means limiting economic growth, too. We must find a solution that supports the economy and also protects people.

Write an essay of 300 – 600 words taking a position on whether the growth of cities should continue in areas vulnerable to storms and flooding. Support your position using logic and examples.

# ESL – Language Use

*Choose the answer that correctly completes the sentence.*

1. The flight _____, so we will have to wait at the airport.
   A) delays
   B) delayed
   C) is delayed
   D) will delay

2. Please _____ your mom today.
   A) calling
   B) calls
   C) called
   D) call

3. _____ the Eiffel Tower when he visited Paris.
   A) They saw
   B) He seen
   C) They seen
   D) He saw

4. Marie Curie received Nobel prizes in Physics and Chemistry for her _____ in those fields.
   A) has researched
   B) research
   C) researching
   D) researched

5. Where _____ you have lunch?
   A) are
   B) have
   C) did
   D) is

6. Sound travels faster in water _____ in air.
   A) than
   B) more
   C) less
   D) at

7. The Great Barrier Reef is the largest living system _____ the world.
   A) for
   B) about
   C) on
   D) in

8. When _____ arrive in the city?
   A) do she
   B) have she
   C) will she
   D) are she

9. _____ take the bus, don't forget to bring your bus pass.
   A) As you
   B) So you
   C) When you
   D) Though you

10. Grace Hopper is famous _____ the first compiler for a programming language.
    A) for having invented
    B) for inventing
    C) her invention
    D) in inventing

11. Because Robert didn't study, he was _____ that his test grade was one of the highest in the class.
    A) disappointed
    B) bored
    C) interested
    D) surprised

12. After the interview, she felt confident that she had impressed the interviewer.
    A) After
    B) During
    C) Later
    D) Before

13. Vero and Joey always help one another with homework, so it is ___ that they will study for the test together this afternoon.

    A) expecting

    B) expected

    C) surprising

    D) surprised

*Select the answer that best combines the two sentences.*

14. Reese loves playing video games. His sister Melody loves playing video games, too.

    A) Both Reese and his sister Melody love playing video games.

    B) Reese and his sister Melody loves playing video games.

    C) Reese loves playing video games and Melody loves playing video games.

    D) Reese and Melody too love to play video games.

15. Aaliyah thought that it might rain today. She packed her umbrella.

    A) Aaliyah thought that it might rain today, packing her umbrella.

    B) Aaliyah thought that it might rain today, so she packed her umbrella.

    C) Aaliyah thought that it might rain today because she packed her umbrella.

    D) Aaliyah thought that it might rain today when she packed her umbrella.

16. The newest book went on sale. We quickly made our way to the nearest store.

    A) We quickly made our way to the nearest store the newest book went on sale.

    B) When the newest book went on sale, we quickly made our way to the nearest store.

    C) Quickly making our way to the nearest store, the newest book went on sale.

    D) We quickly made our way to the nearest store, so the newest book went on sale.

17. Bamboo can grow nearly three feet in one day. Bamboo is a fast-growing plant.

    A) Being a fast-growing plant, bamboo can grow nearly three feet in one day.

    B) After being a fast-growing plant, bamboo can grow nearly three feet in one day.

    C) Bamboo is a fast-growing plant despite growing nearly three feet in one day.

    D) If bamboo is a fast-growing plant, it grows nearly three feet in one day.

18. The fastest land animal is the cheetah. Cheetahs can reach speeds up to seventy miles an hour.

    A) Cheetahs are the fastest land animal, reached speeds up to seventy miles an hour.

    B) After being the fastest land animal, cheetahs can reach speeds up to seventy miles an hour.

    C) Cheetahs can reach speeds up to seventy miles an hour despite being the fastest land animal.

    D) Reaching speeds up to seventy miles an hour, cheetahs are the fastest land animal.

19. The scientific method helps researchers. It helps them focus their studies and test their hypotheses.

    A) The scientific method helps researchers, and it helps them focus their studies and test their hypotheses.

    B) Researchers use the scientific method, and it helps them focus their studies and test their hypotheses.

    C) The scientific methods helps researchers to focus their studies and test their hypotheses.

    D) Researchers focus their studies and test their hypotheses with the help of the scientific method.

20. Malik loves flying kites. Therefore, his father bought him a new kite for his birthday.

    A) Malik loves flying kites, for his father had bought him a new kite for his birthday.

    B) Malik loves flying kites when his father bought him a new kite for his birthday.

**C)** Because Malik loves flying kites, his father bought him a new one for his birthday.

**D)** Because his father bought Malik one for his birthday, he loves flying kites.

21. There was a lot of traffic. She called her boss to tell him she would be late for work.

    **A)** There was a lot of traffic when she called her boss to tell him she would be late for work.

    **B)** There was a lot of traffic, so she called her boss to tell him she would be late for work.

    **C)** After she called her boss to tell him she would be late for work, there was a lot of traffic.

    **D)** She had been calling her boss to tell him she would be late for work before there was a lot of traffic.

22. Emma loved to make chocolate chip cookies. She made them every Sunday for her family.

    **A)** While Emma loved to make chocolate chip cookies, she had made them every Sunday for her family.

    **B)** After making them every Sunday for her family, Emma loved to make chocolate chip cookies.

    **C)** Emma loved to make chocolate chip cookies because she made them every Sunday for her family.

    **D)** Emma loved to make chocolate chip cookies, so she made them for her family every Sunday.

23. Every night Michelle watches the news. She wants to be informed about current events.

    **A)** Every night Michelle watches the news, but she wants to be informed about current events.

    **B)** Michelle stays informed about current events even though she watches the news every night.

    **C)** To watch the news every night, Michelle is informed about current events.

    **D)** Michelle watches the news every night because she wants to be informed about current events.

→ CONTINUE

# ESL – Reading Skills

1. Chapel Hill, North Carolina, is a popular college town. Home to the University of North Carolina, Chapel Hill is populated by students and other young people, giving this town a lively feel. Chapel Hill is famous for its annual street fair, which especially supports local artists—visual artists, musicians, and performance artists. In fact, the town features murals for the public to enjoy on a daily basis. And of course, everyone supports the popular university sports teams.

   According to the passage, Chapel Hill—

   **A)** is home to North Carolina's professional sports teams

   **B)** is where the University of North Carolina is located

   **C)** is not popular with students and other young people

   **D)** is where the University of South Carolina is located

2. Good dental care is important, and everyone can take steps to protect their teeth. First, all people should visit their dentist at least once a year for a check-up and thorough cleaning. Dentists can determine if there are any potential problems with teeth or related health issues. Next, everyone should brush their teeth at least twice a day, and replace toothbrushes every three months. Most people should floss once a day or once every other day. Many people benefit from rinsing after brushing and flossing with fluoride rinses or mouthwashes that fight plaque. Finally, everyone benefits from limiting consumption of sugar, which is harmful to teeth. There are many easy ways to promote dental health.

   What is the main idea of this passage?

   **A)** Brushing your teeth is less important than visiting the dentist.

   **B)** Brushing your teeth is more important than eating less sugar.

   **C)** Taking care of your teeth is important and difficult.

   **D)** Taking care of your teeth is important, but easy to do with a little effort.

3. New York City can be a great place to raise a family. There are lots of parks and playgrounds for children, and plenty of good schools. It is easy for families of any income to get around on foot or using public transportation. Moreover, New York has an abundance of cultural opportunities. With countless museums, galleries, theaters and musical performances year-round, it is one of the most diverse cities in the world.

   What is the main idea of this passage?

   **A)** New York City is a great place to visit.

   **B)** There are more opportunities for children in New York City than for adults.

   **C)** New York City has opportunities for families of different income levels.

   **D)** New York City has many cultural events.

4. In the U.S., the states of the Great Plains include North and South Dakota, Nebraska, Kansas, and Oklahoma. Parts of eastern Montana, Wyoming, Colorado, and New Mexico also fall within the Great Plains, as does northwestern Texas. Historically the Great Plains were home to millions of buffalo, which were hunted by Native Americans. As the United States grew, the land was conquered and buffalo were killed, making way for white settlers who used the land for cattle ranching and eventually agriculture. Railroads allowed farmers to sell their crops in cities more easily. Today, many people have left the states of the Great Plains to pursue careers and livelihoods where opportunities in business and technology are more abundant in major cities elsewhere in the United States. However, new opportunities have appeared in Plains cities like Omaha and Oklahoma City and in the oil and gas industry in North Dakota.

   Which of the following is implied in the passage above?

A) The states of the Great Plains may start growing again thanks to new opportunities in North Dakota and in cities like Omaha and Oklahoma City.

B) Difficulties in North Dakota and in cities like Omaha and Oklahoma City have caused many people to move away from the Plains states.

C) White settlers used the Great Plains for cattle ranching and agriculture.

D) Native Americans lived off the buffalo found on the Great Plains.

5. A government program to offer working mothers extra money for food and childcare supplies is in danger of being eliminated, due to budget cuts. Some women in the community are writing their local government representative to protest these budget cuts. In fact, one local mother is planning to run for Congress herself.

It is likely that the author believes that:

A) The women in the community do not need extra money for food, just childcare supplies.

B) The local government representative cannot help the community.

C) The woman running for office will change the policy as a member of Congress.

D) The women in the community will not be able to change anything.

6. Many people enjoy collecting coins. This hobby requires a strong knowledge of history and of different cultures. Use of coins goes back thousands of years to ancient times, and civilizations around the world have used them as currency. Some coins are very valuable. However, many collectors enjoy studying and collecting these historical objects regardless of their economic value.

Coin collectors—

A) usually make a lot of money from their hobby

B) have a strong knowledge of history and different cultures

C) possess valuable coins that are worth a lot of money

D) have used coins since ancient times

7. The state of Texas was an independent country before becoming part of the United States. Part of Mexico for centuries, Texas was settled by people of European descent coming from the young United States. These settlers eventually rebelled against Mexico, and Texas declared independence in 1836. A decade of political and military conflict would follow; Texas would later join the United States.

The Texan Revolution was led by

A) people of European descent who had settled in Texas from the United States.

B) people of European descent who had settled in Texas from Mexico.

C) people from Europe and Mexico.

D) people from the United States and Europe.

9. Many high school students have temporary jobs during their summer vacations. Summer businesses like ice cream shops, tourist attractions, and swimming pools provide opportunities for teenagers to earn money and learn responsibility during their time off from school. These jobs also offer teenagers the chance to learn skills like accounting, food handling safety, and lifeguarding; these skills can help them in their studies and as they start to consider career paths.

From this passage, a reader can conclude that the author believes that:

A) Summer jobs are good for teenagers who need extra money, but do not offer life skills.

B) Most teenagers would benefit from having summer jobs.

C) Summer jobs do not offer enough money to teens.

D) Summer businesses should be open year-round.

10. Many members of the community go to the neighborhood health clinic for regular medical treatment. The clinic offers free care to children under the age of five, and free counseling in nutrition for children and pregnant women. Some politicians want to cut funding for the clinic, but community leaders have been able to keep it open through grassroots fundraising in

cooperation with local community groups, churches, and private citizens.

*Grassroots fundraising* means—

A) getting money from the government

B) getting money from relatives outside of the country

C) getting money from local people and organizations

D) getting money from big companies

11. Many phone companies offer families annual group rates to save money on telephone, internet and text message charges. However, customers often complain about extra fees that cause their phone bills to be higher than they had expected. Citizens have complained to their government representatives about unfair marketing and trade practices by communications companies in this regard. As a result, some phone companies have begun to simplify their billing practices. In addition, smaller phone companies have emerged that offer prepaid or monthly plans with fewer fees and more straightforward charges.

What is the main idea of this passage?

A) Smaller phone companies are a better option for customers who are upset with big phone companies.

B) Big phone companies treat their customers unfairly.

C) Customers are upset because phone companies have unfair billing practices.

D) Government action and more market competition have forced big phone companies to develop more fair billing practices.

12. Chicago is the third-largest city in the United States. Located on the shores of Lake Michigan, Chicago is home to the Willis Tower, the tallest building in the U.S.; the Art Institute of Chicago, with world-renowned exhibitions; and Wrigley Field, home of the popular (if unlucky) Chicago Cubs, one of America's most famous baseball teams. Chicagoans enjoy cuisines from around the world. And, of course, any given night of the week music lovers can find great jazz and blues performers in the many clubs in this center of American music.

This passage implies that:

A) the Willis Tower is the tallest building in the U.S.

B) Chicago is located on a lake.

C) Chicago is an important center for jazz and blues music.

D) Chicago is not a very exciting city.

13. Toussaint L'Ouverture was the leader of the Haitian Revolution, when slaves in Haiti rebelled against France, eventually winning their freedom and the independence of Haiti. L'Ouverture was a talented political and military leader, and he formed international alliances to support Haitian independence and freedom for the slaves. Although he died before independence was formally declared, his legacy continues as a fighter for justice and freedom.

It is likely that the author believes that:

A) Haiti and France had a good relationship before Haitian independence.

B) Haiti did not have international support in its struggle for freedom.

C) Toussaint L'Ouverture will not be remembered by many.

D) Toussaint L'Ouverture was a great leader worthy of respect.

14. Niagara Falls is a popular destination for tourists. In the summer, tourists can take boats around the spectacular waterfall, and they can spend time exploring the local regions of upstate New York and southern Ontario. The city of Toronto is not far away. During the winter, sometimes the falls freeze over into enormous frozen icicles, amazing visitors. The falls rest right on the border between the United States and Canada, so tourists must remember to bring their passports if they wish to take advantage of all the attractions the region has to offer.

Visitors to Niagara Falls should bring a passport because:

A) Niagara Falls is located on an international border, so interesting attractions may be located in another country.

B) Visitors require a passport if they wish to explore the falls by boat.

C) All visitors need a passport if they would like to travel to Toronto.

D) Niagara Falls is located on an international border, so it is impossible to visit the waterfall without a passport.

15. Roy and Leticia each work two jobs. Roy works for the water company as a technician and drives a taxi at night. Leticia is a medical assistant and takes care of her neighbor's children four nights a week, in addition to watching her own two sons. Once a week, Leticia goes to a medical class at the community college to improve her career opportunities. Both Roy and Leticia go to church on Sundays and participate in church activities on Sunday afternoons with their families.

From this passage, which of these statements can the reader assume?

A) Roy is planning to go to school part-time.

B) Both Roy and Leticia are extremely busy and would probably enjoy a vacation.

C) Roy is worried that he will lose his job with the water company.

D) Leticia does not enjoy spending time with her neighbor's children.

16. The Museum of Natural Science has opened an exhibit about the ecology of the Columbia River Basin. The exhibit includes plants, insects, birds, and mammals that are unique to the Columbia River Basin and explores the changes that have occurred in this delicate ecosystem over the last century. The exhibit has exciting audio-visual presentations. Individual tickets are available on the museum's website, and groups may apply for special ticket prices by calling the museum directly.

According to the passage, individuals can purchase tickets to the exhibit—

A) at the museum

B) for a special price

C) by phone

D) online

17. Nocturnal animals are animals that sleep during the day and are active at night. They may search for food, hunt, breed, fight, play, or do any other activity throughout the night, returning to their nests or lairs at sunrise to rest until sundown, when they come out again. Nocturnal animals are found throughout the United States and Canada and include bats, owls, certain species of cats, foxes, raccoons, possums, and more.

What is the main idea of the passage?

A) Nocturnal animals sleep during the day.

B) Many animals around the world are nocturnal.

C) Nocturnal animals are active at night and common throughout North America.

D) Nocturnal animals, animals that are active at night, are unusual in North America.

# ESL – Sentence Meaning

*Complete the sentence with the correct word or phrase.*

1. The children helped to _____ the laundry.
   - A) hang around
   - B) hang out
   - C) hang on
   - D) hang up

2. After she went to the store, Denise _____ to pick up the laundry.
   - A) need to
   - B) had to
   - C) have to
   - D) will have to

3. Even though he is the _____ kitten of the group, Noodle is the most playful.
   - A) smallest
   - B) smaller
   - C) more smallest
   - D) most small

4. My friend asked me to help her _____ to her new apartment.
   - A) move out
   - B) move through
   - C) move in
   - D) move to

5. I forgot to _____ what you said— would you mind repeating it?
   - A) write over
   - B) write back
   - C) write on
   - D) write down

6. She needed new shoes; the shoes she was wearing were _____.
   - A) worn up
   - B) worn out
   - C) worn over
   - D) worn off

7. Until the 1980s, when teachers arrived from out of state, the best teachers at the school _____ at the university in Seattle.
   - A) were studied
   - B) have studied
   - C) had studied
   - D) will have studied

8. Sheila and Maria hate broccoli; they think it tastes _____ out of all the vegetables.
   - A) the worst
   - B) worst
   - C) the worse
   - D) worse

*Read the sentence(s), then answer the question.*

9. Mia feels under the weather, so she is staying home today.

   Mia feels—
   - A) cold
   - B) sick
   - C) hot
   - D) worried

10. Don't waste time when grading papers for Professor Huang, because she means business.

    Professor Huang—
    - A) is serious about her work
    - B) is angry about business
    - C) is easily angered
    - D) wishes to focus on business instead of schoolwork

11. Josh always cracks me up.

    Josh—
    - A) makes people angry
    - B) makes people uncomfortable
    - C) is friendly
    - D) is very funny

12. Christopher doesn't like visiting family, going on trips, or meeting new people.

Christopher is most likely—

A) lonely

B) boring

C) unfriendly

D) unhappy

13. France is known for its excellent cuisine; tourists often visit restaurants when in the country.

According to the sentence, what is France famous for?

A) tourism

B) food

C) museums

D) art

14. Danny works on and off for his father.

How often does Danny work for his father?

A) regularly

B) on weekends

C) sometimes

D) never

15. Rachel and Jacqueline booked a flight for next Tuesday.

Rachel and Jacqueline—

A) got airplane tickets for Tuesday's flight

B) will buy airplane tickets next Tuesday

C) purchased a book of tickets on Tuesday

D) bought airplane tickets on Tuesday

16. Sara got used to the air conditioning in her office.

Sara—

A) was uncomfortable with the air conditioning

B) did not use the air conditioning

C) began to use the air conditioning

D) became accustomed to the air conditioning

17. Samuel was able to lift more weights than any other man at the gym.

Of all the men at the gym, Sam was the—

A) stronger

B) more strong

C) strongest

D) most stronger

18. Diana meant to call her brother yesterday, but she got busy taking care of the children.

Diana—

A) intended to call her brother

B) did not want to call her brother

C) tried to call her brother

D) was not allowed to call her brother

19. Of all the summers on record, this one has been the hottest.

How does this summer compare to other summers in history?

A) It is less hot.

B) It is about the same.

C) It is the most hot.

D) It is hotter than some, but not others.

20. I promised my mother that I would keep an eye on my little brother.

I promised my mother that I would—

A) look for my little brother

B) watch my little brother

C) find my little brother

D) play with my little brother

21. It is not easy to run a business; you must be organized and hardworking.

It is important to be organized and hardworking—

A) in order to manage a business

B) to easily run from business

C) not to ruin a business

D) in order to do business

# ANSWER KEY

## Arithmetic

| | | | | | | | |
|---|---|---|---|---|---|---|---|
| 1. | B) | 6. | A) | 11. | D) | 16. | B) |
| 2. | C) | 7. | D) | 12. | B) | 17. | A) |
| 3. | C) | 8. | D) | 13. | B) | | |
| 4. | D) | 9. | C) | 14. | D) | | |
| 5. | A) | 10. | C) | 15. | D) | | |

## Elementary Algebra

| | | | | | | | |
|---|---|---|---|---|---|---|---|
| 1. | D) | 4. | A) | 7. | A) | 10. | C) |
| 2. | D) | 5. | A) | 8. | C) | 11. | C) |
| 3. | C) | 6. | C) | 9. | B) | 12. | A) |

## College-Level Math

| | | | | | | | |
|---|---|---|---|---|---|---|---|
| 1. | D) | 6. | D) | 11. | D) | 16. | A) |
| 2. | B) | 7. | B) | 12. | A) | 17. | C) |
| 3. | E) | 8. | A) | 13. | D) | 18. | C) |
| 4. | C) | 9. | B) | 14. | C) | 19. | E) |
| 5. | A) | 10. | C) | 15. | B) | 20. | B) |

## Reading Comprehension

| | | | | | | | |
|---|---|---|---|---|---|---|---|
| 1. | B) | 7. | A) | 13. | B) | 19. | A) |
| 2. | C) | 8. | D) | 14. | B) | 20. | C) |
| 3. | A) | 9. | C) | 15. | D) | 21. | A) |
| 4. | C) | 10. | C) | 16. | A) | 22. | C) |
| 5. | D) | 11. | B) | 17. | C) | | |
| 6. | D) | 12. | B) | 18. | A) | | |

## Sentence Skills

| | | | | | | | |
|---|---|---|---|---|---|---|---|
| 1. | D) | 8. | C) | 15. | C) | 22. | D) |
| 2. | C) | 9. | A) | 16. | B) | 23. | B) |
| 3. | D) | 10. | B) | 17. | D) | 24. | B) |
| 4. | B) | 11. | D) | 18. | C) | 25. | D) |
| 5. | B) | 12. | B) | 19. | A) | | |
| 6. | B) | 13. | B) | 20. | A) | | |
| 7. | D) | 14. | A) | 21. | C) | | |

## ESL – Language Use

| | | | | | | | |
|---|---|---|---|---|---|---|---|
| 1. | C) | 7. | D) | 13. | B) | 19. | C) |
| 2. | D) | 8. | C) | 14. | A) | 20. | C) |
| 3. | D) | 9. | C) | 15. | B) | 21. | B) |
| 4. | B) | 10. | B) | 16. | B) | 22. | D) |
| 5. | C) | 11. | D) | 17. | A) | 23. | D) |
| 6. | A) | 12. | A) | 18. | D) | | |

## ESL – Reading Skills

| | | | | | | | |
|---|---|---|---|---|---|---|---|
| 1. | B) | 6. | B) | 11. | D) | 16. | D) |
| 2. | D) | 7. | A) | 12. | C) | 17. | C) |
| 3. | C) | 8. | C) | 13. | D) | | |
| 4. | A) | 9. | B) | 14. | A) | | |
| 5. | C) | 10. | C) | 15. | B) | | |

## ESL – Sentence Meaning

| | | | | | | | |
|---|---|---|---|---|---|---|---|
| 1. | D) | 7. | C) | 13. | B) | 19. | C) |
| 2. | B) | 8. | A) | 14. | C) | 20. | B) |
| 3. | A) | 9. | B) | 15. | A) | 21. | A) |
| 4. | C) | 10. | A) | 16. | D) | | |
| 5. | D) | 11. | D) | 17. | C) | | |
| 6. | B) | 12. | C) | 18. | A) | | |

# FREE DVD     FREE     FREE DVD

## *From Stress to Success* DVD from Trivium Test Prep

Dear Customer,

Thank you for purchasing from Trivium Test Prep! Whether you're looking to join the military, get into college, or advance your career, we're honored to be a part of your journey.

To show our appreciation (and to help you relieve a little of that test-prep stress), we're offering a **FREE *From Stress to Success* DVD** by Trivium Test Prep. Our DVD includes thirty-five test preparation strategies that will help keep you calm and collected before and during your big exam. All we ask is that you email us your feedback and describe your experience with our product. Amazing, awful, or just so-so: we want to hear what you have to say!

To receive your **FREE *From Stress to Success* DVD**, please email us at 5star@triviumtestprep.com. Include "Free 5 Star" in the subject line and the following information in your email:

1.  The title of the product you purchased.
2.  Your rating from 1 – 5 (with 5 being the best).
3.  Your feedback about the product, including how our materials helped you meet your goals and ways in which we can improve our products.
4.  Your full name and shipping address so we can send your **FREE *From Stress to Success* DVD**.

If you have any questions or concerns please feel free to contact me directly.


Thank you, and good luck with your studies!

**Alyssa Wagoner**
Quality Control
alyssa.wagoner@triviumtestprep.com

# EXCLUSIVE TEST TIPS

Here at Trivium Test Prep, we strive to offer you the exemplary test tools that help you pass your exam the first time. This book includes an overview of important concepts, example questions throughout the text, and practice test questions. But we know that learning how to successfully take a test can be just as important as learning the content being tested. In addition to excelling on the ACCUPLACER, we want to give you the solutions you need to be successful every time you take a test. Our study strategies, preparation pointers, and test tips will help you succeed as you take the ACCUPLACER and any test in the future!

## STUDY STRATEGIES

These are some of the best ways to get the most out of your studying! Whether you're studying with our guides or studying for a class in school with notes you took in class, these strategies will put you on the path to success.

1. Spread out your studying. By taking the time to study a little bit every day, you strengthen your understanding of the testing material, so it's easier to recall that information on the day of the test. Our study guides make this easy by breaking up the concepts into sections with example practice questions, so you can test your knowledge as you read.

2. Create a study calendar. The sections of our book make it easy to review and practice with example questions on a schedule. Decide to read a specific number of pages or complete a number of practice questions every day. Breaking up all of the information in this way can make studying less overwhelming and more manageable.

3. Set measurable goals and motivational rewards. Follow your study calendar and reward yourself for completing reading, example questions, and practice problems and tests. You could take yourself out after a productive week of studying or watch a favorite show after reading a chapter. Treating yourself to rewards is a great way to stay motivated.

4. Use your current knowledge to understand new, unfamiliar concepts. When you learn something new, think about how it relates to something you know really well. Making connections between new ideas and your existing understanding can simplify the learning process and make the new information easier to remember.

5. Make learning interesting! If one aspect of a topic is interesting to you, it can make an entire concept easier to remember. Stay engaged and think about how concepts covered on the exam can affect the things you're interested in. The sidebars throughout the text offer additional information that could make ideas easier to recall.

6. Find a study environment that works for you. For some people, absolute silence in a library results in the most effective study session, while others need the background noise of a coffee shop to fuel productive studying. There are many websites that generate white noise and recreate the sounds of different environments for studying. Figure out what distracts you and what engages you and plan accordingly.

7. Take practice tests in an environment that reflects the exam setting. While it's important to be as comfortable as possible when you study, practicing taking the test exactly as you'll take it on test day will make you more prepared for the actual exam. If your test starts on a Saturday morning, take your practice test on a Saturday morning. If you have access, try to find an empty classroom that has desks like the desks at testing center. The more closely you can mimic the testing center, the more prepared you'll feel on test day.

8. Study hard for the test in the days before the exam, but take it easy the night before and do something relaxing rather than studying and cramming. This will help decrease anxiety, allow you to get a better night's sleep, and be more mentally fresh during the big exam. Watch a light-hearted movie, read a favorite book, or take a walk, for example.

# PREPARATION POINTERS

Studying isn't the only way to get ready for a test. Some of the biggest hurdles can be the prep work that you do before walking into the testing room. Feel cool, calm, and collected by preparing for your tests the right way.

1.  Preparation is key! Don't wait until the day of your exam to gather your pencils, calculator, identification materials, or admission tickets. Check the requirements of the exam as soon as possible. Some tests require materials that may take more time to obtain, such as a passport-style photo, so be sure that you have plenty of time to collect everything. The night before the exam, lay out everything you'll need, so it's all ready to go on test day! We recommend at least two forms of ID, your admission ticket or confirmation, pencils, a high protein, compact snack, bottled water, and any necessary medications. Some testing centers will require you to put all of your supplies in a clear plastic bag. If you're prepared, you will be less stressed the morning of, and less likely to forget anything important.

2.  If you're taking a pencil-and-paper exam, test your erasers on paper. Some erasers leave big, dark stains on paper instead of rubbing out pencil marks. Make sure your erasers work for you and the pencils you plan to use.

3.  Make sure you give yourself your usual amount of sleep, preferably at least 7 – 8 hours. You may find you need even more sleep. Pay attention to how much you sleep in the days before the exam, and how many hours it takes for you to feel refreshed. This will allow you to be as sharp as possible during the test and make fewer simple mistakes.

4.  Make sure to make transportation arrangements ahead of time, and have a backup plan in case your ride falls through. You don't want to be stressing about how you're going to get to the testing center the morning of the exam.

5.  Many testing locations keep their air conditioners on high. You want to remember to bring a sweater or jacket in case the test center is too cold, as you never know how hot or cold the testing location could be. Remember, while you can always adjust for heat by removing layers.

# TEST TIPS

You've made it to the testing room! It's almost time to put all of your hard work to the test, literally. Good luck!

1. Go with your gut when choosing an answer. Statistically, the answer that comes to mind first is often the right one. This is assuming you studied the material, of course, which we hope you have done if you've read through one of our books!

2. For true or false questions: if you genuinely don't know the answer, mark it true. In most tests, there are typically more true answers than false answers.

3. For multiple-choice questions, read ALL the answer choices before marking an answer, even if you think you know the answer when you come across it. You may find your original "right" answer isn't necessarily the best option.

4. Look for key words: in multiple choice exams, particularly those that require you to read through a text, the questions typically contain key words. These key words can help the test taker choose the correct answer or confuse you if you don't recognize them. Common keywords are: *most, during, after, initially,* and *first.* Be sure you identify them before you read the available answers. Identifying the key words makes a huge difference in your chances of passing the test.

5. Narrow answers down by using the process of elimination: after you understand the question, read each answer. If you don't know the answer right away, use the process of elimination to narrow down the answer choices. It is easy to identify at least one answer that isn't correct. Continue to narrow down the choices before choosing the answer you believe best fits the question. By following this process, you increase your chances of selecting the correct answer.

6. Don't worry if others finish before or after you. Go at your own pace, and focus on the test in front of you.

7. Finally, Relax. With our help, we know you'll be ready to conquer the ACCUPLACER. You've studied and worked hard!

Keep in mind that every individual takes tests differently, so strategies that might work for you may not work for someone else. You know yourself best and are the best person to determine which of these tips and strategies will benefit your studying and test taking. Best of luck as you study, test, and work toward your future!

CPSIA information can be obtained
at www.ICGtesting.com
Printed in the USA
LVOW09s1921310317
529202LV00008B/344/P